Politics and Religion in Contemporary India

Politics and Religion in Contemporary India

Edited by
Ishwar Modi

RAWAT PUBLICATIONS
Jaipur • New Delhi • Bangalore • Hyderabad • Guwahati • Kolkata

ISBN 978-81-316-0668-1

This volume draws upon articles published in the special issue of the journal *Politics and Religion*, Vol. VII, No. 1/ 2013.

Published by
Prem Rawat for **Rawat Publications**
Satyam Apts, Sector 3, Jawahar Nagar, Jaipur 302 004 (India)
Phone: 0141 265 1748/7006 Fax: 0141 265 1748
E-mail: info@rawatbooks.com
Website: www.rawatbooks.com

New Delhi Office
4858/24, Ansari Road, Daryaganj, New Delhi 110 002
Phone: 011 2326 3290

Also at *Bangalore, Hyderabad, Guwahati* and *Kolkata*

Typeset by Rawat Computers, Jaipur
Printed at Chaman Enterprises, New Delhi

Contents

Introduction

When Dr Miroljub Jevtic, the Editor-in-Chief of the prestigious journal *Politics and Religion* published by the Center for Study of Religion and Religious Tolerance, Belgrade, Serbia invited me to guest edit its special issue of the journal focusing on 'Politics and Religion in India', my initial reaction to accepting this challenging responsibility was not favourable since I never thought I had the requisite specialized expertize either in political sociology or in sociology of religion or else in the interface and interplay of politics and religion. However, friendly persuasion and persistence of Dr Jevtic and his reminding me that I have already put in the word of guest editor to their issue on 'Secularism versus Religion' way back in 2009, I was hardly left with any other option but to accept his invitation. To begin with, I was reluctant to accept this prestigious offer knowing well that in spite of the continuous play and interface between politics and religion in India, where all sorts of political parties exist with very different ideological orientations having no inhibition in justifying the use of religion for their political benefits and fortunes, it would not be easy to have a good number of contributions for this special issue since at this moment not many senior sociologists are engaged in these areas of research in spite of their utmost importance. However, quite a few very senior and other scholars of sociology who had been engaged and are still working on these issues, accepted my invitation to contribute papers in order to help me realize this invitation. I am thankful to all of them.

It is a matter of great pleasure and honour for me that this particular issue of *Politics and Religion* is entirely devoted to some of the important aspects of society, polity and religion in India. The aspects covered in this special issue are important not only historically but also in the contemporary context. Whatever has been included in this volume will certainly provide a window to the world, and more so to the European, particularly to the East European and Balkan sociologists, to have a glimpse of the contemporary Indian scenario mainly in the context of politics and religion, their interplay and particularly the construction of varied identities based on religion and other social factors such as caste, community and gender.

C.N. Venugopal in his paper 'Polity, Religion and Secularism in India: A Study of Interrelationships' observes that the Indian political systems have been traditionally guided by two types of juridical texts: (i) The *dharmashastras* (composed by Manu and others); (ii) The *nitishastras* (such as Kautilya's *Arthashastra*, Shukra's *Nitisara* and Bhisma's address to the princes in *Mahabharata* which is known as *Shantiparva*). The texts of the first type laid down rules for conducting sacred duties, codes of conduct, punishment for transgression. The texts of the second type deal with more mundane matters related to agriculture, irrigation, imports and exports and military organization. It is here that Indian secularism originated. In other words, the rulers protected both sacred and secular pursuits of their subjects. The Indian rulers (Hindu, Buddhists and Jaina) followed the same texts in administering justice, conducting warfare against the invaders and maintaining internal peace. Venugopal further observes that the two ancient systems of Indian philosophy – *Vaisheshika* and *Samkhya* were highly ratiocinative. They laid the foundations for developments in Indian science. Alburini, the Persian scholar, described in detail India's developments in science, mathematics and astronomy in the 10th century AD. This clearly shows that Indian religions have not opposed science which is a secular activity. The Indian constitution (1951) has not seen any contradiction between religion and secularism. Both types of activities are legitimate in India. All people of India have freedom of worship; only condition is that one religious group should not interfere in the religious life of another group. However, in the recent years the Hindu, Sikh and Muslim militant groups have not only arisen but have also disturbed the social harmony. It has led to the politicization of religion. These tensions and problems have been more fully analysed in his paper.

Taking this debate to a higher-level Ananta Kumar Giri in his paper 'The Politics of Religion and the Complex Spirituality of Religious Encounters and Co-Realizations: The Multiverse of Hindu Engagement with Christianity in India' discusses the complexity of spiritual quest and border-crossing dialogues in India. It discusses the multiverse of engagement between Hindus and Christians and the plural streams of co-walking, contradictions and confrontations. It discusses the complex histories of encounters between Hindus and Christians and also discusses the inter-religious dialogues undertaken by religious leaders, reformers and common people from both the traditions.

While Hindu–Muslim encounters and interrelationships and also the questions of Muslim identity have almost continuously been talked about and examined by the social scientists in India, much less attention has been paid to the construction of Sikh identity. Paramjit S. Judge in his paper 'Community Within Community: Politics of Exclusion in the Construction of Sikh Identity' examines the construction of religious identity among the Sikhs from the socio-historical perspective. It has been argued that the Sikh identity was constructed as a result of the colonial intervention in which the emphasis turned to the appearance instead of faith as such. The new identity was a product of the politics of the times and it was perpetuated in order to maintain the hegemonic domination. Sikhism, despite its egalitarian ideology, failed to create a casteless community. Discrimination and exclusion of lower castes continued. An empirical investigation into the conditions and perceptions of the lowest caste, namely Mazhabi, clearly demonstrated their exclusion, whereas discourse of equality among the Sikhs is used to create a moral community. Despite the equality of worship among the Sikhs, the Mazhabis at the local level are denied the equal religious rights in the *gurdwaras* (Sikh temple) owned and controlled by the upper dominant castes. Judge suggests that the roots of the exclusion have to be located in the history of the making of the religious community and the way a few castes after benefiting from religious conversion perpetuated the caste-based exclusions.

While the paper by Judge focused on the construction of Sikh identity, the paper by Ashish Saxena and Vijaylaxmi Saxena on 'Religious Landscape, Low Caste Hindus and the Identity Politics: Configuration of Socio-religious Space for Weaker Sections in Jammu City, J&K (India)' focuses on low caste Hindus and the identity politics. Their paper explores the spatial expansion of subaltern groups in urban setting; socio-religious mobility among lower caste Hindus and the creation of sacred and secular space vis-à-vis higher Hindu caste groups in a sacred traditional Indian city. The broader findings of their paper reflect the creation of religious spaces and also the lower caste Hindu identity assertion through these places. The modern forces and the pace of urbanization had diluted the airtight compartmentalized segregation of the weaker section and paved them way for secular living with the other high caste groups. They hold that it had not only brought democratic dwelling space but also provided them dignity with the new level of assertion.

It can hardly be overemphasized that the questions of identity of the various groups of people based on religion, caste, community, and even gender have become a focal point of many sociologists and other social scientists while dealing with the questions of politics and religion in contemporary India. Ajay I. Choudhary in his paper 'Buddhist Identity: A Case Study of Buddhist Women's Narratives in Nagpur City' focuses on a much less examined and explored area of research. He has examined Buddhist women's identity in the broader context of Buddhist identity. Choudhary holds that Dr Ambedkar's conversion to Buddhism had succeeded to a great extent in providing a new respectable identity to many. Yet the status of Buddhist women, among the Buddhist community, remained the most unexamined part of this conversion. His paper tries to examine whether the Buddhist identity succeeded to provide a sense of self respect and equal status to Buddhist women or to what extent the Buddhist identity was able to replace their stigmatized identity in public sphere by investigating the narrative provided by the Buddhist women about their own identity.

Going beyond the complex interface between politics and religion, the paper by Ramanuj Ganguly 'Social Dynamics in a Religious Milieu: The Sevayats of the Jagannath Temple at Puri' mainly focuses on the *Sevayats* of one of the oldest and most prominent temple, i.e. Jagannath temple at Puri, who are the ritual functionaries of the temple. Ganguly informs us that the *Sevayats* have survived and emerged as the most faithful and the truest upholders of this enigmatic religious tradition for around nine centuries in the face of social, economic and political ups and downs. His paper tries to describe in today's context, their socio-economic status, their view about themselves and the temple, and their position in the temple and the society. His paper is not intended to provide a historical account of the temple, nor does it try to analyse the temple as a whole. Looking at the broader society, the paper tries to establish the linkages between the *Sevayats* and the greater society, and how the *Sevayats* are responding to the broader forces of change. The focus is on the nature of the changing organization and functioning of the *Sevayats*, where the past has been used only as a point of reference.

The paper by Susan Visvanathan 'Sacred Rivers: Energy Resources and People's Power' is a good mix of how several important aspects of life – the socio-religious, the secular and the economic, as well as the legal and political – can merge and interplay with each other in the broader context of a sacred river which can meet people's energy requirements. Her paper is primarily concerned with the way energy requirements in the last three decades have seen a response from local communities who wish to express their love and longing for traditional occupations. Agriculture is a multi-faceted representation, and riverine civilizations have epitomized the relation between land, labour and production not just as a relation with technology and culture, but also in terms of the symbols of the sacred. With large-scale over-utilization of resources and a lack of vision, the rivers are polluted. People's movements draw on the work of scientists and those working in the Arts, including the Humanities and the Social Sciences, to draw attention to the way in which petitions and protests communicate that politics is not merely about imposing 'the good vision from above' but is an interplay between the political, the legal, the socio-religious, the secular, and the economic. In a democracy, politics is essentially about dialogue, and the rate of industrialization may well be mediated by the power of the greens and environment movements, which have learnt their lessons from genocide of peasantry and tribals, and the mass exploitation of the resources of nature. Susan Visvanathan has attempted to document some of the shifts and evolving positions in this ongoing debate in India.

It is not only a matter of honour for me to be associated with *Politics and Religion* but also a matter of satisfaction and pride that India is drawing renewed attention of the international community of sociologists and other scholars. I do hope that this special issue of the journal will provide better understanding of society, polity and religion and their interface in India, and also generate further interest among overseas scholars to study Indian society.

Ishwar Modi

Contributors

Ajay I. Choudhary, Hislop College, Nagpur, India. E-mail: ajaychou@gmail.com

Ananta Kumar Giri, Madras Institute of Development Studies, Chennai, India. E-mail: aumkrishna@yahoo.com

Ashish Saxena, Central University of Allahabad, Allahabad, India. E-mail: ashish.ju@gmail.com

C.N. Venugopal, Jawaharlal Nehru University, New Delhi, India.

Ishwar Modi, President of Indian Sociological Society; Director of India International Institute of Social Sciences, Jaipur; Executive Committee Member of International Sociological Association. E-mail: iiiss2005modi@yahoo.co.in

Paramjit S. Judge, Guru Nanak Dev University, Amritsar, India. E-mail: paramjitjudge@yahoo.co.uk

Ramanuj Ganguly, West Bengal State University, Barasat, Kolkata, India. E-mail: rg.wbsu@gmail.com, rg.wbsu@yahoo.in

Susan Visvanathan, Jawaharlal Nehru University, New Delhi, India. E-mail: susanvisvanathan@gmail.com

Vijaylaxmi Saxena, Ex-lecturer, Calliope Law College, University of Jammu, Jammu, India.

1

Polity, Religion and Secularism in India

A Study of Interrelationships

C.N. Venugopal

The Indian subcontinent was a welter of many political experiments. In the millennium preceding the Christian era, the northern India was dotted with many small states called the *ganarajyas* (republics). These were the autonomous states, with an elective monarchy, a designated territory, a royal court, and the soldiers entrusted with a security of the domain. These republics were reminiscent of the ancient city states of Greece. In the Buddhist text *Dighanikaya* there are references to such states. Similarly, in the Buddhist Jataka tales three are references to them. Buddha and Mahavira, the great religious reformers, were born into the royal clans of such republics. In these texts there are indications that the incompetent or wicked ruler was thrown out by his angry subjects and he was replaced by a new ruler. In the 3rd century BC, the Greek warrior Alexander started from his Macedonian kingdom and carried out a successful military operation against the Persian rule. He reached Punjab (the border of India) and soon after returned to his kingdom, but he passed away during this journey. His brief stay near India led to a socio-political ferment, which stirred up India's nationalistic aspirations. In north India a Brahmin pundit, named Chanakya (also known as Kautilya) mobilized the masses of people, by alerting them about the threat of foreign invasion. He inspired a warrior (Chandragupta) who rallied people around him, raised an army and overthrew the corrupt rulers of Maghadha (Bihar) and set up the Mauryan kingdom. He closely followed Chanakya's advice in launching an Empire, which in course of time controlled a vast territory in north India. The Greek ambassador in the Mauryan court, Magsthenes, put on record his detailed observations of Chandragupta's rule. In this large state irrigation, agriculture, mining, trade, and commerce were actively promoted and controlled by centralized administration.

The small republics mentioned above were nearly obliterated by the march of large states. This was inevitable because a centralized rule was needed to defend India's vast territory. The Indian society had always existed on the basis of the varnashrama dharma which was a four tier social system. As such there was no Hobbesian state in India. The king or the ruler was the one who protected this social system and enforced sacred and social regulations among the members of society. There was no divine right theory in Indian kinship. This is because the king was not the source of law. His authority to rule was based on the juridical texts known as (a) Dharmashastra – composed by Manu and others, and (b) *nitishastras*.[1] These texts are written in Sanskrit and they have guided the rulers of ancient India: Hindu Buddhist and Jaina. The texts of the first type dealt with sacred aspects of life, enforced ritual obligations on the people and also prescribed expiation to those who violated the rules. Even if the king was not Hindu he did not interfere in the ritualistic life of his subjects. In particular, the dharmashastras[2] enjoyed upon the ruler to uphold the varna order by wielding the sword if needed.

The king's punishment of those who transgressed the rules was usually preceded by expiation. Besides, the karma theory widely accepted in India held that the wrong doers would incur demerits in the next round of births. The folk tales of India mention that the ruler often moved among the common people incognito in order to know the true state of his policies. Chanakya insisted that the ruler should be a model of good conduct to his subjects. He should be available to the common people and exert himself for the welfare of the state. His famous work *Arthshastra*[3] belong to the second type of text known as nitishastra. There are three other well-known individuals, namely Shukra, Bhisma and Vidura, who contributed to the nitishastra. These texts are not directly concerned with sacred aspects. They do emphasize that moral behaviour must be maintained. The old traditions need to be followed. However, they are also concerned with secular governance. The people must pay taxes to the state and contribute to economic production.

Ashoka who became the ruler of Mauryan empire was personally a Buddhist but extended his protection to Brahmins and Jainas. In his royal edicts engraved on stone he declared that he had undertaken welfare measures for the common people. In his realm roads were laid, trees were planted, water sources were created, rest houses were constructed for travelers, and hospitals for human beings, animals and birds were set up. He extended his patronage even to the tribals who lived in the forests. More than this he was available to the common people most part of the day and night. Of course, as a Buddhist he forbade the killing of animals for food. He set a personal example by greatly reducing consumption of meat in his palace. This measure made him unpopular among some people. He sent peace missions to Greece, Iran and Sri Lanka. H.G. Wells, writer and historian, has said that there was no greater monarch than Ashoka in history. The Buddhists called him Chakravartin (wielder of the moral wheel) and thus placed him on a high pedestal.

An interesting aspect of Indian rulership is that although the king wields the sword in order to punish the offenders, yet he has no personal motive, hatred or anger. As the Nordic Indologist Unto Tahtinen was shown the king emerges as a non-violent person.[4] In other words he remains mentally non-violent even while discharging his military duties. The Latin phase sine ira et studio (without anger and passion) aptly describes a state of mind. In fact the Hindu sacred texts such as epics, the purans and Bhagavad Gita uphold the kings' duty in maintaining social order by the use of force or military action. This trend was reversed with the rise of Buddhism which made the ruling classes give up arms and turn inward. At the turn of the 10th century AD India's borders became more vulnerable to foreign invasions. In sum, the Indian ethos did not uphold a policy of non-violence but expected the rulers to be free from personal hatred towards the wrong doers.

In the southern peninsula during the first two millennia after Christ, there was an extensive growth and spread of village councils known as panchayats. Theses councils of common people governed small areas of rural India. They controlled land, water sources, forests, etc. The Panchayats collected fines from the rule breakers and also prescribed expiation. They settled caste disputes in open assembly. The southern rulers such as Chola, Pallava, Pandya, Chera, etc. did not interfere in the panchayats. But the criminal disputes were beyond the scope of panchayats and the king's court had to intervene in such cases. There was a wide participation of the villagers – men, women and children – in the meetings organized by the panchayats. Sir Henry Maine, the British jurist, called them the Village Republics. India attained freedom in 1947 and became a republic in 1950, all these years democracy as a social system had worked well in India; the elections are fair and free. The masses of India are not educated. In spite of this, the people have exercised a good judgement in electing their representatives to the assembly and the parliament. They have been occasionally misled by corrupt politicians; yet sooner or later they have shown a capacity to elect the right person. These political skills have been inherited due to the legacy of the panchayats which flourished in the north upto the 10th century AD and in the south upto 17th century AD. At present panchayat system has been under the shadow of the big political parties. A revival of this system will be a very valuable aid to strengthen democracy at the basic level of Indian society.

The modern Indian secularism has taken off from the past and as such retains the elements from previous times. Most of the rulers (foreign or Indian) adopted a policy of tolerance towards different faiths. The Greeks, Kushans, Muslims, and British who ruled at different times in the form of small kingdoms or as a big empire usually gave grants and endowments to temples, mosques and churches. During British times, Lord Curzon established Archaeological Survey of India in the early part of the 20th century for the protection and preservation of national monuments. This was a major step which led to the discovery and protection of Hindu, Buddhist, Jaina, Sikh, Muslim, and Christian monuments. There were two noted archaeologists, namely Sir John Marshal and Sir Mortimer Wheeler who left deep a imprint on the others who continued their work. Also the British government established a muzarai (religious endowment department) in the government, to give grants for the upkeep of temples, etc. All these policies and practices have continued up to the present in free India. Today, major Hindu temples are managed by government offices. Likewise, the religious places are generally under the control of government especially in different states of the Indian union. When the major festivals of different communities are held large numbers of people participate in them. The state police and paramilitary forces have controlled the crowds. One example is Kumbha Mela which is held in north once in 12 years. Millions of people participate in this event. Unless the state employs its security agencies, these events cannot remain free from mishaps. Therefore it is quite clear that the Indian state which is secular in the sense that it is not based upon any particular religion, is nevertheless actively engaged in protecting the people's religious interests. The central assumption is that even if the state does not believe in religion, most of the common citizens believe in it. Hence, the state extends its supports to the religious events. Another important policy is that the religious establishments controlled by the government are open to all people irrespective of their religious affiliation. If discrimination is reported then the grants given to the temples, etc. is suspended. Besides, there are various religious boards which regulate the activities of their respective places of worships.

In India there are numerous schools and colleges run by Hindu, Sikh, Christian, and Islamic groups. Mainly they teach secular course and subjects. There are also medical, engineering and management colleges run by the various trusts. In so far they help in the spread of education, they are recognized by the government and receive grants. The examinations are conducted by the various government agencies. Thus there is an interdependence between private and public wings of the society. In sum, secularism in India is more practical than ideological. In some western countries religion is treated as a personal or private matter. This is not the case in India even if the Indian constitution has separated religion from secular activity.

In the Indian schools and colleges people of different faiths get education. For instance, the Banaras Hindu University is opened to non-Hindus also. Likewise, Catholic schools and colleges admit many non-catholics. There is no religious instruction in these institutions which implies indoctrination. The religious trust retain control over the selection of the staff members subject to the common qualification laid down by the educational boards of the government. It must be mentioned here that the government at the state and central level has embarked upon extensive spread of education. This effort is supplemented by private enterprise mentioned above. In the early part of 20th century Banaras Hindu University was brought into existence by the efforts of Annie Besent (an Irish person) who worked with the Indian nationalists. The Christian missionaries spread education in south-central and south-eastern tribal areas on a large scale during the last few decades. Still there are large sections of people who are not educated. The public literacy campaigns have not been successful, because there is a belief among some sections of people that formal education does not make much difference to them.

Religion in Indian Society

The major Indian religion such as Hinduism, Buddhism and Jainism belong to the pantheistic system; similarly, the minor religions also share the same belief. This is also found in Japan, China and other countries of the Far East. In these religions there are multiple ties between man and nature. In fact, the nature's diversities such as water, earth, hills, valleys, sea coasts are believed to be permeated by divinity. The Hindu reach far away Mount Kailash which is located between India and China to offer their prayers to it. Likewise, the Japanese reach top of Mount Fuji for prayer and worship. Even the flora and fauna are part of the sacred order. The lotus flower is regarded as sacred in many parts of Asia. The Hindu God Vishnu rides garuda (eagle) as his vehicle; Shiva rides a bull and the Goddess Durga rides a lion. The Indian society is not polytheistic because its divinities are not discrete entities but arise from the same transcendental source. For example, the numerous gods and goddesses of popular Hinduism are all derived from the three primal deities Shiva, Vishnu and Shakti. The Muslims and Christians who came to India were unable to understand that there was oneness in the manifold idols or icons which were worshipped in Indian homes and temples. The early Muslim invaders destroyed the temples thinking that idolatry was thriving in them. The idols are only personifications of some symbols or ideas which are intangible in nature. These symbols are like the archetypes described by C.G. Jung in his study of the collective unconscious.

Inclusiveness has always been the hallmark of pantheism. In India many religions have lived side by side, in spite of occasional communal strife. In Japan Shintoism has lived side by side with Buddhism; in China Confucian, Tapist and Buddhist beliefs and practices are commonly shared by the people. In the monotheist religions of West Asia divinity was withdrawn from the nature and made transcendental. Under this system what one believes in or adheres to is subjected to control by the religious doctrine. A Hindu may worship a personal deity of his choice – even Jesus Christ! It does not disqualify him provided he gets along with others in performing rituals, or at least in participating in religious functions. In a pantheistic setting no one ever disputes the existence of god in academic terms. Therefore, a person who does not believe in god is not called an atheist but an agnostic. As a rule Buddhists and Jains are agnostic: they do not subscribe to the creation of the world by divine decree. The agnostic attitude is this: 'I do not know why or how this has happened'. An agnostic nevertheless firmly believes in an underlying spirituality.

There are important aspects of religions in India: (a) places worship; (b) monastic institutions; and (c) sects and cults.

(a) *Places of Worship:* The number of holy places (temples, church, mosque) found in India is legion. Patronage by private donors, public donations and voluntary labour by local community have provided the mans to build them. They are the centres where people gather to offer prayers and participate in collective events. They have lend grandeur to India in lasting way. The lingaraj temple of Orissa, the Khajuraho temples of Orissa, the Kailas temple of Ellora in Maharashtra, and the Brihadeeswara temple of Tamil Nadu are just a few examples. The Buddhist stupa at Sanchi (M.P.), the Jaina temple of Mount Abu (Rajasthan), the Golden temple of Sikhs in Amritsar (Punjab), the Bahai Temple in New Delhi, the Swami Narayan Temple of Ahmedabad are some of the holy places of the Indian sects old and new. Likewise the cathedrals of old Goa (now part of India), the Islamic Monuments in Agra, Delhi and Bijapur (Karnataka) are also impressive monuments. The impact of these places of worship on people is two fold: (1) Religious and (2) Cultural. Already reference has been made to the religious aspect. The second type of experience is available to the visitor who may be a non-believer but admires the vast and varied cultural dimensions of India. Associated with the places of worship is the pilgrimage in which people move across the country in order to visit the sacred centres.

Pilgrimage is an universal type of movement among people of many countries who seek religious or spiritual solace. They traverse vast distances on land or sea to reach a holy place. Prior to modern transport pilgrims endured much physical exertion to fulfill their desire. There were also many difficulties faced by them in getting food, shelter and water. Still for centuries the pilgrims carried out their vow to visit the holy places. Jerusalem, Santiago and Banares are a few of the places which have attracted pilgrims from all over the world. Victor Turner (the British social anthropologist) have done outstanding work in his comparative study of pilgrimage.[5] In India people from south move to far reaches to north to worship a mountain or take bath in a holy river. Likewise, the people of north visit the sea coast of western India or south India for a religious purpose. The improvement in transport and communication in India have lent help to the pilgrims. Even today the pilgrims have to stay in crowded shelters and endure many personal discomforts. In the northern religion landslides and floods occur in the Himalayan range during monsoon months. The cold season in the north is also very severe. These difficulties have not stopped pilgrims from their march. The pilgrims include both individuals and groups who share food and shelter during the journey and make no complaints about the drawbacks.

One outstanding outcome of pilgrimage in India and elsewhere is the pervasive sense of equality among the participants. When thousands of men, women and children take bath in holy rivers or in hot water springs near the temples there is no concern about their ethnic or caste background. The usual identity which come from the village or caste background is obliterated during the journey. The deeply structured inequality of the society is countered by the anti-structure of the assemblage of people at a holy place. The pilgrimage is valuable guide to the understanding of Indian society. It serves as a much needed corrective to the assumption that India is dominated by hierarchic notions which limit the interactions among the people and promote barriers. In fact in Hindu temples the caste distinctions are not dominant. The priest who conducts rituals for the people is not necessarily a Brahmin. In some of the important temples of India there are Brahmins as well as non-Brahmins. Normally, the castes are separated from each other and are marked by auspiciousness. For example, a non-Brahmin who is ritually impure but is trained in temple liturgy acquires an auspicious status. Hence, the temples also come under the category of anti-structures. In the scholarly writings on Indian society undue emphasis is placed on caste inequality. A totalistic understanding is more helpful for reaching a balanced depiction of India. The holy men and women of India have come from diverse castes but due to their inner attainment they are placed far above the ordinary men and women, no one thinks of their caste status; those who are in search of solace come to them on their own.

Among the non-Hindus durgahs of Muslims and gurudwaras of Sikhs have served to make India a more equal society. They have given shelter to people irrespective of their religious background. They are found in many parts of India and they are visited by people from diverse backgrounds. In a country where poverty, natural calamities and warfare have made people destitude or homeless such havens have given hope and provided concrete help. The temples, durgahs and gurudwaras, the basic level, are organizations of people's welfare. Unlike the political policies of welfare which are subject to fluctuations, these welfare centres have consistently catered to the needs of people. It is mainly by the public donations which are voluntary that these are managed. Besides, no publicity campaign is launched by a holy place to secure advantages from people. The visitors who come to these centres seek the blessings to heal their sickness or find a solution to their personal problems. The continuation of traditional mode of welfare in modern times is a noticeable fact. Thus, tradition and modernity have impinged on each other.

(b) *Monastic Institutions:* Buddhism and Jainism in some respects differed from the main doctrine of Hinduism. Both of them aimed at a non-ritualistic kind of religion. The Buddhist and Jaina approach was to promote an ascetic orientation by instilling monastic discipline[6] among their followers. Later, in the 8th century AD Shankara (the Hindu reformer) started 10 orders of ascetics. The monks and nuns in Buddhists and Jaina monasteries engaged themselves in prayer, meditation and learning. Similarly the Hindu monastic orders reoriented the life of the people by eliminating some rituals and practices. Max Weber, in his study of religions, referred to the otherworldly attitude of India. He was mainly looking at the ascetic attitude of the monastic. He overlooked the fact that there was diversity in India. The ascetic were no doubt very important but there were many other sections of society who did not share this attitude. Centuries ago in India made progress in astronomy, mathematics, metallurgy, ship-building, etc. The Indian traders were engaged in trade even outside India including Greece and Rome. The Buddhist monasteries which were thriving on the Silk Route, which connected India to Central Asia on the one hand and Far East on the other hand, served as shelters for the traders and also provided warehousing facilities for their goods; they even provided banking facilities. The Hindu monastic orders extended educational opportunities to the people at large. In the last few decades the Arya Samaj, the Ramakrishna Mission, the Swamy Narayan Trust, and the Lingayat Educational Society have done extensive educational work in India, while keeping firmly their commitment to monastic values and norms.

An important aspect of monasticism is that there is scope for any aspirant to attain a high spiritual status through the ascetic path. For example, the four noted exponents of India's spirituality, namely, Vivekanda, Yogandanda, Sri Aurobindo and Mahesh Yogi belonged to a non-Brahminical background. There is a wrong impression in some quarters that the Brahmins escaped from the caste restrictions and became dominant in the monasteries. In fact the ascetic or monastic path is open to every one. There is no doubt that the ascetics have valourized the Indian society.[7] Swamy Vivekananda inspired generations of Indians by his teachings which called upon the people to rebuild the Indian Society. Sri Aurobindo made a painstaking study of the Rig Veda and cleared the mental cobwebs created by the Western indologist. He showed that the Vedas were a rich source of symbols and ideas which can help in the reconstruction of India. Incidentally, both of them were traditionalists and did not derive from modern reforms. According to them the sanatana dharma yielded more and more insights for reconstruction of the present and the future if there is sufficient introspection. The monastic orders have also published extensively on Indian culture and religion in English and other languages. The objective of social service through education and inculcation of discipline among the youth has been achieved by these missions.

A brief reference may be made here to the Christian monasteries. In medieval Europe a number of monastic orders founded by Jesuits, Benedictines, the followers of St. Francis started ameliorative work. These orders were opposed to the worldly concerns of the Roman Church during the Dark Age of Europe, these monastic centres were enclaves of learning and spirituality. They encouraged the cultivation of sciences and arts within the cloisters. The educational missions derived from them are found in India also. There are many convents, schools and colleges named after St. Charles, St. Zavier, Lady of the Rosary, etc. While the Catholics have gained a firm roothold in the domain of education, the Protestants are actively engaged in the spread of medical welfare through hospitals. India's composite societies is built up many cultural strands but there is an underlying unity which seems to be timeless.

(c) *Castes, Sects and Cults:* Castes and their Networks: In the post-Vedic times for several centuries have occupied a dominant position in India. There are about 3000 castes, small or big. The all India pattern recognizes four varna orders: the learned people, the warriors, traders and agriculturists and the service class. But verna (which means colour) is different from jati (caste). The verna refers to a national category based on the individuals attributes; by contrast jati refers to a concrete category into which one is born. There have been several kings or soldiers who came up from non-warrior background but attained success due to self-effort. For example, Chandra Gupta was born into a non-ruling family; yet he became the emperor through his valour. Likewise a person born in the lower category can rise to the rank of the learned. Valmiki who composed Ramayana and Vyas who composed Mahabharata came up from a lower level. The castes[8] are hereditary social unit. At the time of birth a person acquires a social position high or low. It is called 'status by ascription' in sociology. However, many castes arose from the guild background. The guilds were engaged in the production of weapons, textiles, arts, and crafts. The productive process in the country was supported by the guilds. Their rulers assured protection to the castes and guilds by confirming their traditional rights and privileges. This policy measure helped in the continuation of social order.

Castes shared from positive as well as negative traits. They conferred a social identity on their members. Marriage, property inheritance and peaceful pursuit of occupations were made possible under the aegis of caste framework. The main difference between the higher and lower castes is this: the former are usually affiliated to the monastic orders from whom they seek guidance; the latter have strong caste councils which strictly regulate the conduct of their members. The negative aspects of castes are the exclusive attitude of their members. There are also ritual restrictions which limit the psychological barriers in daily life. Due to modernization some of these restrictions are modified but within the closed circle of caste they continue in one way or the other. But virtually all spheres of life professions, services, political affiliations are influenced by castes in some way or other. When the candidates contest the elections for the assembly or the parliament, caste and community consideration have a role to play. However, there are exception to this rule. It must be recognized that the reality of caste has somewhat halted India's secular progress.

Castes in India cut across the religions barriers. In some form or the other caste consideration are present among the Muslims, the Sikhs and the Christians. Among the non-Hindu groups castes are not recognized in terms of doctrine or spiritual authority. But they exist as ground reality: Marriages are not devoid of caste ties. The converts from upper castes prefer their own level in choosing the marriage partners. Louis Dumont, the French sociologist, has made references to the pervasive caste consciousness in India. In the recent years, the lower castes have acquired some special status in the form of quotas in admission to colleges, jobs, etc. The sects which exist in India are in principle different from castes but they too have some caste preferences. But in modern times the castes are interacting in public places (markets, etc.) as never before. The old social isolation does not exist any longer. In buses and trains people move together, take food in hotels without reference to the caste background. This is a step in modernization.

Sects and Cults: The last millennium saw the rise of devotional movements called Bhaktism.[9] In every major region of India, the Bhakti movement emphasized the common man's nearness to god through the emotions of love, affection and goodwill. Guru Nanak in Punjab, Tulsidas and Kabir in the Hindi region of north India, Chaitanya Mahaprabhu in Bengal, Basaveswara in Karnataka, Shankardeva in Assam, Mira Bai in Rajasthan, and Narsi Mehta in Gujarat are some of the examples. These people ware poets and saints who composed in the regional languages which were commonly understood by the people. The modernization of Indian languages was made possible by such literary efforts. Even to this day they are popular because people can understand the message. These poets came from the diverse backgrounds. Tukaram who composed Marathi literature of high order came from a lower caste. The Bhakti movement liberated people from the hegemony of Sanskrit. In fact this contributed to the secularization of Indian society by opening up the common channels of communication.

Another important outcome of the Bhakti movement was that the social interactions among the people were no longer restricted to the caste background. The satsang organized under the aegis of Bhaktism were assemblages of people in which men, women and children prayed together, ate the food served to them and also stayed in common shelters. For centuries the satsangs have occupied an important place in north India. The satsangs are similar to pilgrimage: just as the bath in the holy river purifies a person, the participant in a Bhakti gathering is purified; the guru male or female is the holy water. Similarly, the Sufis of north India rallied people around them irrespective of their caste or community background. Both Bhakti and Sufi social gatherings ushered in widespread syncretistic culture in India. The Hindu and Muslim groups shared many values by participating in devotional activities.

The sects lay down some criteria for admitting members to their fold. The members have to abide by the discipline of the sect. They have to wear clothes and share the food according to the common practices. The sect membership confers on them a social identity which is distinct from caste identity. In the sect the Guru is succeeded by a designated discipline who is acceptable to the members. By contrast, in a cult the people rally around a person credited with mystical or magical powers. After this person is no longer there, the cult usually ceases to exist. However, the followers of cult believe that the spirit of the leader exists in transcendental sense. For example Shirdi Saibaba who existed in the last part of 19th century in Maharashtra has become the cult figure of an extraordinary stature. Even now numerous people converge in the shrine dedicated to him and offer prayers to him. The cult is growing stronger by the day; the modern transport had aided the fast movement of people from different parts of India towards Shirdi. Similar cults are existing in India which attract a wide variety of people. Common to cults is the magic or miracle which is attributed personality of the cult leader.

Secularism has become the main trend in modern world. In Western Europe after the industrial revolution, many countries separated state from Church in the public domain. The state adopted secular policies independent of the Church. Thereafter religious affairs became part of private domain. One reason for this was that the Church resisted some developments in science; besides the people were experiencing a lack of mental freedom because they had to abide by the doctrine of the Church. In Western Europe secularism reached the zenith in France after the French revolution; along with the march in science and technology mass political parties arose in Europe which nearly obliterated the earlier political pluralism based on local communities. Noted intellectual[10] like Durkheim, Bonald,

Hegel, and Edmund Burke resisted the inroads made by the big political set up. The previous political system was based upon primary human relations in which people knew each other. The social solidarity based on reciprocity and collective feelings was eroded by an impersonal political culture.

In India there has never been a separation between the secular and the religious domain in historical as well as present times. The noted rulers of the past such as Ashoka, Kanishka, the Imperial Guptas, and Harsha who controlled most parts of north India had followed a policy of tolerance toward religions. They made grants and donations to Hindu, Buddhist and Jaina temples and monasteries. During the Islamic rule (11th to 17th centuries AD) there were some mixed trends. Some of the early sultans used forces to convert sections of people to Islam. Aurangzeb the later Moughal ruler imposed upon non-Muslims a religious tax known as Jizya. But Akbar was a liberal ruler who brought together Hindus and Muslims through his amity and goodwill. The British rulers of the early period of colonialism were not opposed to India's religious traditions. Warren Hastings the governor general sent his offerings to the temple of kali in Kolkata worshipped by Hindus. He also gave grants to Max Muller to edit and translate the Rig Veda from Sanskrit into English. The sultans and kings who ruled in India generally tolerated religious diversities because it ensured for them the loyalty of their subjects.

Under the constitution of India there are provisions for both secular and religious pursuits; individuals and groups are free to follow their chosen way of life without, of course, curtaining each other's right. B.R. Ambedkar who contributed much to the making of the Indian constitution became a Buddhist and launched a social movement for the improvement of the underprivileged groups in India. He used a religious idiom in guiding his followers on the path of progress. He generally encouraged education for the masses. M.K. Gandhi who led the people of India to political freedom was a religious person. He drew his ideas from Gita, Bible and Koran. In the 1950s Vinoba Bhave, a follower of Gandhi, launched the

Sarvodaya Movement to redeem the plight of the landless peasants and other deprived sections. He too used ideas drawn from religious texts to awaken the people and draw them out of their backwardness. Both Gandhi and Bhave gave attention to the improvement of rural life through constructive programmes. Thus secular progress is not halted by the religious orientation; even if the leaders of the society are non-believers, most common people subscribe to one faith or the other.

The communal strife which occurred in India before and after Independence was the result of the British policy of divide and rule. In the first decade of the 20th century Lord Curzon the viceroy of India divided Bengal into Western and Eastern provinces by the communal criteria. This created a discord between Hindu and Muslims. In North India communal electorates were created in which the Hindus and Muslims voted separately in the provincial elections. This later led to the creation of India and Pakistan as separate states in the region. In the post Independence period the communal riots took place in many towns and cities in which both Hindus and Muslims were killed. At present communal strife has receded to the background but the national unity is disrupted due to militancy and terrorism. One positive trend is that the religious bodies which have been part of the Indian tradition have not become communal in outlook. By contrast both among Hindu and Muslim militant groups have given rise to a communal ideology in other words, there is communalization of some sections of political parties but the religious groups are not similarly affected.[11]

There are two challenges to secularism in present day India. One is that there is a long standing dynastic tradition in Indian society, during the British rule, which lasted for nearly two and half centuries (18th century to the middle of 20th century). Under the treaty relations six hundred princely states were created all over India. The traditional ruling families who became the heads of these states were given special powers and privileges. In turn most of these rulers remained loyal to the British Empire. They lived in large palaces and led a lavish life style which was supported by their inherited wealth and a large share of the taxes collected from their subjects. In contrast most people in these states lived in poverty, controlled by their caste regulations. However a few large states like Hyderabad, Baroda, Indore, Bhopal, Jaipur, and Mysore became quite progressive in terms of education, industrial development, etc. The succession to these states was inherited right subject to the viceroy's approval. Between 1947 and 1950 most of these states were merged in the Indian union but the former rulers retained some privileges till the year 1971.

In many spheres of Indian society such as politics, business, professions such as law and medicine, defense services, etc. usually the offspring continue in the path of their elders. In the professions and the defense services selection is through competition and those who are not up to the mark cannot get into them. But in politics and business merit alone is not sufficient to succeed to top position. Here nepotism and favouritism came into the selection process. The rules may be modified to accommodate smooth succession. The persons endowed with merit suffer a setback because of extraneous influences. In the development of Indian secularism this method is unsuitable. In the field of business there is an emergence of crony capitalism in some areas of investment. This means that business partnerships are made or broken not according to the market criteria but according to family, kinship and caste considerations. This has adversely affected the further development of Indian industry. It is worth mentioning that during the long colonial rule there was no comprador capitalism. The Indian business houses such as Tatas, Birlas built up capital through their hard work and public support. They did not derive capital from the British banks. The Indian banking industry which has contributed to the emergence of industries has remained strong till the present. In contrast in USA many small or big banks have gone into liquidation. Since the 1980s India has become self sufficient in grains due to important strides made in the techniques of production. The emergence of a large middle class has altered India's position in the world. In spite of poverty and backwardness which are evident in the country's hinterland it has reached the status of a high order.

A brief reference may be made to the prevalence of corruption in public life. American sociologist Sutherland's description of white collar crime is found in India also. This type of crime is not visible to the public but it leads to diversion of public funds, misuse of official position for selfish ends and formation of secrete networks. The respectable looking politician, administrator or businessman has often indulged in corruption. In particular the funds are diverted into the hands of kith and kin for safe custody. In the recent years some very big cases of corruption have been exposed through the mass media, there is also a lot of protest against corruption by the members of the public. In the coming years this will be a big challenge for Indian society. Among the common people there is an appreciation of the British rule where most of the foreign and Indian officers and subordinates were dedicated to their work and maintained clean records of service. When there is a fast development of the country there is a higher incidence of corruption due to the lack of effective supervision. There is a negative trait among many Indians who treat corruption with indifference. Further the lack of corrective action has come in the way of eliminating corruption.

Notes

1. There were also instruction systems in Sanskrit known as vidyas (which were composed between 1st and 5th century AD). These were used for the training of young members of the ruling class in various arts and sciences. Both sacred and secular subjects were included in them. Vedas, Astronomy and Archery were among the subjects studied by the pupils. See G.S. Ghurye, 'Vedas' in his work *Anthropo-Sociological Papers*, Popular Prakashan, Bombay, 1963, pp. 303–51.
2. Ananda Coomaraswamy (noted commentator on Indian culture) writes: 'The emergence of a definitely Brahmanical rather than a Buddhist scheme of life is to be attributed to the fact that the practical energies of Buddhists were largely absorbed within the

limits of monasticism. The Buddhists in the main regard Nirvana ... as the sole object of life. But the Brahmans never forgot that this life is in the field alike of Pursuit and Return. Their scheme of life is set forth at great length in the Sutra literature, the Dharma Shastras and the Epics (in general 4th–1st centuries BC). See his work, *The Dance of Shiva*, Munshiram Manoharlal, New Delhi, 1975 (Indian Reprint), p. 42.

3. See A.K. Sen, *Hindu Political Thought*, Gyan Publishers, New Delhi, 1986 (Indian Reprint), pp. 135–79.
4. See Unto Tahtinen, *Non-Violent Theories of Punishment*, Motilal Banarsidass, Delhi, 1983.
5. See Victor Turner, *The Ritual Process: Structure and Anti-Structure*, Aldine, Chicago, 1969.
6. P.A. Sorokin referred to the stoic discipline practiced in the European monastic orders. He wrote: 'The majority of the medieval thinkers stressed the same idea in various ways partly in the form of various philosophies and psychological theories, but principally in the form of the applied arts of the re-education human beings successfully practiced in the monasteries and similar institutions.' See his work, *Contemporary Sociological Theories*, Kalyani Publishers, New Delhi, 1978 (Indian Reprint), p. 602.
7. (a) See G.S. Ghurye, *Indian Sadhus*, Popular Prakashan, Bombay, 1964. (b) C.N. Venugopal, 'G.S. Ghurye's Sociology of Religion', in A.R. Momin (ed.), *The Legacy of G.S. Ghurye*, Popular Prakashan, Bombay, 1966, pp. 47–60.
8. Berreman writes: 'A caste hierarchy is to large extent an interactional hierarchy ... Every relevant other is a superior, a peer or an inferior depending on caste. Only within the caste is status equality found ...' See his work, 'Caste Systems', in Peter Worsley (ed.), *Modern Sociology*, Penguin, Harmondsworth, UK, p. 511.
9. (a) See C.N. Venugopal, *Ideology and Society in India*, Criterion, New Delhi, 1988. (b) C.N. Venugopal, *Religion and Society in India*, Gyan Publishers, New Delhi, 1988.
10. See Robert Nisbet, *The Sociological Tradition*, Basic Books, New York, 1966, pp. 47–106.
11. See C.N. Venugopal, 'The Sociology of Religion in India', in Yogendra Singh (ed.), *Social Sciences: Communication, Anthropology and Sociology*, Pearson Longman, New Delhi, 2010, p. 485.

References

Ahmad, Q., 1983, *Indian Al-Biruni*, National Book Trust, New Delhi.

Chopra, Deepak, 2008, *The Third Jesus*, Rider Publications, UK.

Ananyananda, Swamy, 1971, *The Teachings of Swami Vivekananda*, Advaita Ashram, Mayavati, Almora.

Aurobindo, Sri, 2000, *India's Rebirth*, Institute for Evolutionary Research, Mysore, India.

Hettiarachchi, Shanthikumar, 2007, 'Tamil Tiger "Martyrdom" in Sri Lanka: Faith in Suicide for Nationhood?', *Politics and Religion Journal*, Vol. 1, No. 2.

Hussain, Abid, 1973, *India's National Culture*, National Book Trust, New Delhi.

Jevtic, Miroljub, 2007, 'Political Science and Religion', *Politics and Religion Journal*, Vol. 1, No. 1.

——, 2008, 'Religion and Relations between Genders', *Politics and Religion Journal*, Vol. 2, No. 1.

Joshi, Kireet, 1994, *The Veda and the Indian Culture*, Rashtriya Veda Vidya Pratishthan, Delhi.

Sharma, A.K. (ed.), 2011, *Essays in Honour of Professor C.N. Venugopal*, D.K. Printers, New Delhi.

Sharma, Vishwanath, 2004, *Chanakya Niti*, Manoj Publications, Delhi.

2

The Politics of Religion and the Complex Spirituality of Religious Encounters and Co-Realizations

The Multiverse of Hindu Engagement with Christianity in India

Ananta Kumar Giri

To be a good Hindu also meant that I would be a good Christian. There was no need for me to join your crowd to be a believer in the beauty of the teaching of Jesus or try to follow his example.

— Mohandas Karamchand Gandhi

But how many churches are willing to worship Krishna or Siva as the same universal God described in the Bible? [...] Jewish and Christian religions cannot afford to compromise on their history-centric beliefs, because to do so would be tantamount to surrendering their claim of unique access to knowledge of God's will.

— Rajiv Malhotra (2011), *Being Different: An Indian Challenge to Western Universalism*, pp. 23–93

The Christian of the future will be a mystic, or else no Christian at all.

— Karl Rahner (1973), 'The Spirituality of the Church of the Future', p. 149

The Upanishads open to the Christian world the farther horizons of something of the mystery of the Divine. If one's mind is open to the mystical quest of the Upanishads one cannot be fixated on the particular form of God's revelation, nor can one be dogmatic about the concrete formulations in theology. [...] In this unending spiritual pursuit the Christian theologian meets the Hindu Vedantin; the interpretation of the spiritual dynamics of the New Testament is deepened by the mystical insights of the Upanishads. The anthropocentric worldview of Christianity is balanced by the cosmic world-view of the Upanishadic sages; the emphasis on rituals is harmonized with the pursuit of contemplation; the social initiatives get integrated with ecological concerns. [...]

A similar encounter and deepening process takes place in the Hindu encounter with Christian faith. There are prophetic streams in Hindu scriptures and socio-critical initiatives in Hindu traditions. But under the weight of Brahmin domination and caste structure these have not been sufficiently articulated in the process of social transformation. The concerns of equanimity (*samadarsana*), solidarity (*yajna*), integral welfare (*kshemam*), justice (*dharma*), and good for all (*sarvabhutahiteratah*) have often been neglected or even suppressed. The prophetic literature of the Bible and the liberative message of Jesus could help Hindus discover this social transformative potential of God-experience.

— Sebastian Painadath (2007),
We are Co-Pilgrims, pp. 74–75

The term 'Christian' is more of an adjective than a noun. The term [...] is a property of something else, a concept that implies 'diminishment' – which is indicative of positional subordination. [...] there was never such a thing, nor is there any such thing as a purely 'Indian' Christian, any basic or generic sense. Only more earth-bound, 'hybrid,' or 'hyphenated' forms of Christians can be implied within historical understandings. Such Christians were, and are, pinned to the earth by their local culture and languages – and most of all, by their birth (*jat*), or caste.

— Robert Eric Frynkenberg (2010),
Christianity in India: From Beginnings to the Present, p. 458

The Politics of Religion and the Complex Spirituality of Religious Encounters and Co-Realizations

The relation between politics and religion is a complex one in any society as it is the relationship between religion and power, religion and spiritual quest, and spirituality and power. While religion is much more entangled with a politics of domination and control, spiritual quest, along with its equally complex entanglement in politics, is a much more open-ended journey of self-realization, co-realization and struggle for beauty, dignity and dialogues in self, culture, society and the world. The politics of inter-religious encounters is different from spiritual encounters of religions as the later is much more open-ended and is accompanied by complex processes of co-learning, co-realizations and confrontations. In Indian histories and contemporary societies, we see this complex process at work. In my paper, I discuss this with regard to the multiverse of Hindu Christian engagement in India.

Hinduism and Christianity have been in interaction for a long time. According to some, Jesus and his spiritual journey which later took an institutional form in Christianity was deeply influenced by devotional streams in Vaishnavism and spiritual quest in Buddhism prevalent in India and Asia. Jesus himself is said to have come to India and Tibet during the missing years of his life in Palestine and learnt the art of yoga and spiritual quest (see Yogananda 2007).[1] Many fellow seekers and fellow pilgrims such as Ramakrishna Paramahansa, Paramahansa Yogananda and Swami Vivekananda have realized in Jesus a yogi, a spiritual master and an embodiment of Divinity and have found great affinity between inclusive streams of yoga in India and Asia and the spiritual quest of Jesus. On a related historical note, since the time of the Apostles, Christianity has been with India. St Thomas is said to have come to India, preach among the people and was tragically murdered. But since then his followers and their community have been part of Indian social and religious life. Then with the Portugese colonial conquest of Goa, it opened up new limits and possibilities of evangelism, colonialism and cross-cultural denigration, confrontation and mutual challenge.

Complex Histories of Co-Walking from the Hindu Shores

With the Portugese colonial conquest of Goa, Western Christianity got a new lease of life in India. Robert de Nobili (1577–1656) came to India after this as part of Jesuit missionary activities. He accepted indigenous mode of dressing and behaved as a Hindu sanyasi. But, as Amaladoss tells us, 'He adopted local customs in order to win over the people of his day and to communicate his message, and not necessarily because he appreciated these customs' (Amaladoss et al. 2005: 33).

When we come to the modern period, we see the deep significance of encounter with Christianity in the reforms of Hinduism and formation of challenging streams such as Brahma Samaj. But even before this, encounter with Christianity had influenced Bhakti movements in India and varieties of critical spirituality which had challenged caste and feudal domination. As Gail Omvedt writes: '[…] While it may appear unrealistic to argue that Kabir's 'sai' was actually 'Isa' (Jesus) and make him into a kind of crypto-Christian, it remains quite possible that among the later poets using the name 'Kabir' one was indeed influenced by Christian ideas. After the sixteenth century, specifically after 1545 when Jesuits began to spread through north and south India, a wide compact of ideas can be seen. In Maharashtra, a Krista Purana was reported as composed in 1626, as one of the earliest Konkani/Marathi writings, written by Fr. Thomas Stephen (1549–1619), an English Jesuit […]' (2008: 65).

Rammohan Roy (1772–1833), considered by many as the father of modern Bengal-Indian Renaissance, was influenced by the ethical precepts of Jesus. As Romain Rolland writes: 'Roy extracted from Christianity its ethical system, but rejected the divinity of Christ, just as he rejected the Hindu incarnations' (Rolland 1954: 103). He was also influenced by Islam, its lack of idolatry and monotheism. In fact, his first book was on Islam entitled *Tuhfat-ul-Muwathiddin* (A Present to the Believers in One God; a treatise in Persian with a preface in Arabic language). Roy's encounter with Christianity made him realize the ethical significance of religion and with this he wanted to fight against cruel practices in Hinduism such as *Sati*. His interpretation of Christianity was challenged by evangelical and doctrinaire Christians of the time such as Marshman who insisted on the significance of baptism and dogma. But in this insistence, Christianity lost a chance to creatively engage itself with the ethical and wider challenges of society beyond doctrinaire assertion and dogma. Unfortunately the situation is not much different now even after two hundred years.[2]

Keshab Chandra Sen (1838–1884), Roy's successor in Brahmo Samaj, continued the creative dialogue with both Hinduism and Christianity but he sought to bring devotion to Roy's rationalism.[3] If Roy had missed dialogue with indigenous devotional stream of Bengal and India such as the great Chaitanya movement which had transformed the religious situation in medieval India, making it anti-caste and open to dialogue with Islam, Keshab brought the Chaitanya stream to Brahmo Samaj thus widening the social base of Brahmo Samaj.[4] In this, he would have been definitely influenced by his meeting with Sri Ramakrishna though some also think that Keshab also influenced Ramakrishna.[5] Keshab introduced a new form of worship in the mother language (cf. Mukherjee 1992). Keshab wrote creatively in both Bengali and English and he contributed to a new style in Bengali prose which would have brought him closer in his communication and interaction with ordinary people of Bengal.[6]

In his engagement with Christianity, Keshab offered his own concept and realization of Oriental Christ: 'Behold! He cometh to us in his long flowing garment, his dress and feature altogether Oriental' (quoted in Thomas 1970: 70). Keshab also focused on the need to develop indigenous Christianity and develop a national church which is Christ-centred, rather than narrowly church-centred. What Thomas had written more than forty years ago on Keshab's vision is still a challenge before Christianity in India, Asia and the world:

> [...] the idea of a Christ-centered integration of the Indian and Western religious and cultural heritages, expressing itself in an indigenous Christianity, is highly relevant to the future of

> the Christian church in India. In fact, the Church of South India has written into its constitution that it stands for a Church expressing the universality of Christ in indigenous thought-patterns and life-forms of the Indian people. In view of the rapid changes taking place in these thought – patterns and life-forms, it is necessary to say that the church must become indigenous not to an India that is past, but to contemporary India in which the religious and cultural traditions of its hoary past are themselves seeking reintegration within the context of the new humanism relevant to the developing secular, pluralistic and open society.[7]

P.C. Mazoomdar (1840–1905), Keshab's successor in Brahmo Samaj also followed his theme of Oriental Christ. For Mazoomdar, if 'the light of Oriental Christ and mystic devotion is allowed to fall upon the 'ecclesiastical figure of the Sweet Prophet of Nazareth, that figure will be 'illumined with strange and unknown radiance' (quoted in Thomas 1970: 83). Along with his realization of Oriental Christ, Mazoomdar also laid emphasis on the significance of Holy Spirit in life and the world. His emphasis on Spirit also brings us to a similar emphasis by Bede Griffiths[8] from the other side of the shore though, for Thomas, Mazoomdar reduces 'the Trinity to a Spirit-monism' (ibid.: 99).

In the mulitverse of Hindu engagement with Christianity in 19th century Sri Ramakrishna (1836–86) and Swami Vivekananda (1863–1902) have been deeply influential. Sri Ramakrisna's realization of Jesus and Madonna was a spiritual realization going beyond dogma and outward paraphernalia. Once Ramakrishna saw a picture of Madonna in one Jadu Mallick's country house and he was immediately moved by it. After this he also realized the presence of Jesus.[9] Ramakrishna was also deeply moved by the Biblical story of Peter walking on water: 'A picture of this scene was later hung on the wall of his quarters in the temple; it was the only image that was borrowed from the Christian tradition' (Schouten 2012: 87).

Swami Vivekananda 'was formed by the mystical experience of his teacher' (ibid.: 82). For him, 'The best commentary on the life of [Jesus] is his own life'. 'The foxes have holes, the birds of the air have nests, but the Son of Man has no where to lay his head.' That is what Christ says as the only way to salvation; he lays down no other way.' He writes about Jesus: 'He had no other occupation in life, no other thought except that one, that he was a spirit. [...] And not only so, but he, with his marvelous vision, had found that every man and woman, whether Jew or Gentile, whether rich or poor, whether saint or sinner, was the embodiment of the same undying spirit as himself. Therefore, the one work his whole life showed was to call upon them to realize their own spiritual nature. [...] You are all Sons of God, immortal Spirit. 'Know', he declared, 'the Kingdom of Heaven is within you.' 'I and my Father are one.' Dare you stand up and say, not only that 'I am the Son of God,' but I shall also find in my heart of hearts that I and my Father are one?' (Vivekananda 2011: 21).

Swami Vivekananda realizes Jesus as a Son of the Orient and Christianity as a religion from Asia and the Orient.[10] Like many from India, he is not bothered about the historicity[11] of Jesus but realizes Him as God: 'If I, as an Oriental, have to worship Jesus of Nazareth, there is only one way left to me, that is, to worship him as God and nothing else' (ibid.: 23).

Unlike Rammohan Roy, Swami Vivekananda looks at Sermon on the Mount as not primarily ethical; he was not impressed by the 'moral precepts of the Sermon on the Mount. [...] He once called the famous Golden Rule, with which the Sermon on the Mount ends, 'excessively vulgar' because of the orientation to the Self. For him, the heart of all religion was to transcend the orientation to the self and to achieve unity with the godhead. One text in the Sermon on the Mount stood out, in his view, i.e. 'Blessed are the pure in heart for they will see God' (Schouten 2012: 98). But from this it is not helpful to make a contrast between ethical Christ and mystical Christ in Swami Vivekananda.[12] Swami Vivekananda was deeply influenced by the ethical and practical work of Jesus as his mystical and spiritual work. He was concerned with ethical aspects of religion and society and in their transformation through what he called practical Vedanta. As Thomas aptly puts it: '[…] it is possible to look at Vivekananda's religion as an attempt to synthesize Advaita Vedanta with Christian philanthropy […]' (1970: 246). But Vivekananda's practical Vedanta was not just philanthropy; it was also an engagement in practical mysticism as it was with Sri Ramakrishna. In fact, Sri Ramakrishna brought the challenge of transformation of suffering as the central challenge before any religion, and especially Hinduism, and it is said that he once kicked Swami Vivekananda in his mouth to make him realize that he should not just hanker after his own salvation, rather work for the amelioration of suffering such as poverty and transformation of the world.[13]

It is the realization of Jesus which had played a key role in the formation of Sri Ramakrishna Mission. Swami Vivekananda founded the order telling to his fellow walkers the story of Jesus Christ.[14] Seekers in Sri Ramakrishna-Vivekananda stream have continued to undertake their own journey of Jesus realization and formally Christmas is a holiday in Sri Ramakrishna mission – a tradition started by Swami Brahmananda who succeeded Swami Vivekananda. This has inspired some Hindus such as Vengal Chakkarai who was a prominent Christian nationalist and theologian to embrace Christianity.[15] Of many monks from Sri Ramakrishna Mission who have written about Christ such as Swami Akhilananda who wrote *Hindu View of Christ*, Swami Ranganathananda's *Christ We Adore* calls for our own co-walking realization of Jesus. Like Swami Vivekananda, for Swami Ranganathananda, 'The Kingdom of God is within you' has 'extraordinary significance for Hindus' (Schouten 2012: 100). As Schouten tells us: 'Ranganathananda also interprets 'within you' as 'in your inner self': the Kingdom of God can be experienced in the inner life. Pureness in heart is a precondition for sharing in this kingdom. But whoever fulfils this condition can realize unity with God and thus see God' (ibid.: 100).[16] Thus encounter with Christianity in Ramakrishna-Vivekananda stream was a decisive step in the shaping of modern Hinduism which also led to much deeper and wider turns and cross-currents of reconstruction, creativity and confrontations (confronting one's tradition as Swami Vivekananda had done) compared to what had happened during the days of Brahmo Samaj.[17]

Paramahansa Yogananda (1893–1952), the spiritual seeker from India who has inspired millions across the world also realizes Jesus as a yogi and a spiritual teacher.[18] Philosopher S. Radhakrishnan (1888–1975) realizes Jesus in terms of sacrifice of ego.[19] This also finds a resonance in the Christian theological interpretation of Christ and Trinity which also realizes the significance of sacrifice (cf. Anand 2004). For instance, Drawing inspiration from Vedic notion of Purusa as Jagnya, Subhash Anand develops a notion of Trinity and God as Self-giving: '[…] the Father is the Father because He gives himself totally to the Son; the Son is the Son because He gives himself totally to the Father; and the Spirit is precisely this […] mutual self-giving […]' (Anand 2004: 45). He presents similar views of Swiss theologian Hans Urs von Balthasar:

> Father's self-utterance in the generation of the Son is an initial 'kenosis' within the Godhead that underpins all subsequent kenosis. For the Father strips himself, without remainder, of his Godhead and hands it over to the Son […] Inherent in Father's love is an absolute renunciation: he will not be God for himself alone. He lets go of his divinity (ibid.: 46).

The theme of sacrifice brings us to Gandhi's (1869–1948) realization of Jesus, engagement with and challenge to Christianity. Gandhi realized Jesus as a *Satyagrahi* and in his engagement with and challenge to Christianity realized cross in societies and histories. Many Christians realized Gandhi's non-cooperation movement and freedom struggles as bearing cross[20] for liberation while others sided with the imperialist and colonialist forces. S.K. George was one such Christian who was inspired by Gandhi's non-cooperation movement of 1919–21 and took part in it which 'made real to his youthful mind the idealism and passion of Jesus of Nazareth' (Thomas 1970: 219).

'And in the Civil Disobedience Movement of 1930–32 he felt his Christian duty 'to appeal to all Indian Christians to join in and act as custodians of non-violence' (ibid.). 'But for this he not only lost his job in the theological college in Calcutta where he was teaching but his affiliation with church.' But he was not deterred by this and lived his life for realization of satyagraha and an 'undogmatic Christianity' (ibid.).[21]

George took part in India's freedom struggle but he was not alone. Many Christians took part in India's freedom struggle.[22] In his book, *Gandhi's Challenge to Christianity*, George tells about Gandhi as a spiritual fact[23] having demonstrated 'how the Sermon on the Mount can be practical politics' (1939: 25). In his foreword to this book, Radhakrishna also writes: 'Whatever the Continental theologian may say, it is impossible for the Indian Christian to resist the impression that God has been present in the age-long struggle of man for light. The fact of Gandhi is a challenge to the exclusive claims of Christianity' (ibid.: 9).[24]

In his engagement with Christianity, Gandhi was deeply influenced by Sermon on the Mount[25] and he found similarity between the Sermon and the Gita. Gandhi was also influenced by Tolstoy's understanding of Christianity.[26] In his journey of life Gandhi felt 'great leaning to Christianity and for a time wavered between Christianity and Hinduism. But in the end, he saw no reason for changing his religion' (Thomas 1970: 210).

Gandhi was opposed to conversion to Christianity using gullible means. His first priority was reform of one's religion. Gandhi's critique of conversion raised issues of responsibility to reform one's religion of birth but his was not a closed approach to one's own religion as he himself was wavering between Hinduism and Christianity seriously considering to convert to the later at one time.[27] But Bishop Azariah, the Bishop of Dronakal, challenged Gandhi's view on conversion by arguing that conversion is not only led by foreign missionaries but also by people like himself who had grown up from the soil of suffering and was working with them for their amelioration and transformation.[28] But Gandhi's opposition to conversion is not an instance of what Omvedt (2008) calls his 'soft Hindutva'. She is here swayed away by her own judgmental enthusiasm and seems not to try to understand Gandhi's own position as well as his border-crossing realizations. As the above paragraph says, Gandhi was not relating to Christians only as a Hindu, he was seeking to realize himself as simultaneously Hindu, Christian, Muslim, Buddhist, and many more.[29]

In tune with many spiritual seekers from Hinduism and India whom we have discussed in the previous pages, Deepak Chopra (2008: 9) presents us his realization of a Third Jesus 'who taught his followers how to reach the God-consciousness'. For Chopra, 'The first Jesus was a rabbi who wandered the shores of Northern Galilee many centuries ago' (ibid.: 8). The second Jesus is a product of theological construction what Rajiv Malhotra (2007) calls the Nicean creed: 'Millions of people worship another Jesus, however, who never existed, who does not even lay claim to the fleeting substance of the first Jesus. This is the Jesus built up over thousands of years by theologians and other scholars. He is the Holy Ghost, the Three-in-One Christ, the source of sacraments and prayers that were unknown to the rabbi Jesus when he walked the earth' (ibid.: 9). Chopra further writes: 'The idea of the Second Coming has been especially destructive to Jesus' intentions, because it postpones what needs to happen now. The Third coming – finding God-consciousness through your own efforts – happens in the present' (ibid.: 10).

To this multiverse of Hindu engagement with Christianity, we can invite realizations of Chittaranjan Das (1923–2011), a creative thinker from Odisha. In his 'Jesus Christ, White, Black or Yellow?' Das tells us: '[…] whatever might be said about the Jesus in history, Jesus has come to be one of the very important inspiration in mankind's history and continues to be that inspiration even today' (2012: 27). Like many of his fellow seekers, Das urges us to go beyond a merely historicist understanding of Jesus and here urges us to realize the mystical quest of Meister Eckhart: 'For Eckhart, Jesus was not born only once at one particular point of history. He is being born every moment of our life and world's life. […] Jesus ceases to be only a happening in history, he becomes a challenge instead [...]' (ibid., also see Mieth 2009). But to realize this we need to go beyond the theological construction of Jesus including the Papal condemnation of life of poverty of Jesus.[30]

Hindu Christian Engagement: From the Shore of Christian Journey

As Hindus have realized Jesus and Christianity with their own initial starting points in a journey of unfolding realizations, so have Christians who have sought to understand not only Hinduism but also Jesus and Christianity with an immersion in some of the spiritual pathways of Hinduism. Here we can begin with the journey of Jesus himself. It is believed that Jesus himself came to India and Tibet during the missing years of his life in Palestine and learnt from the spiritual practices of these lands. Both the devotional stream of Krishna and the Vaishnavas and the spiritual seeking of Buddhism influenced Jesus.[31] Down the ages Christians have been influenced by their participation in the cultural and spiritual journey of Hindus which unfortunately has also meant retaining or adapting one's caste practice.

Like our previous section, here we can focus on a few exemplary voices their working with what Victoria Harrison (2011) calls 'exemplary reasoning.'[32] We come right to the modern period and begin with Brahmabandhav Upadhyaya (1861–1907). Upadhyaya was a classmate of Swami Vivekananda. He accepted Christianity and was baptized. He also took part in the Swadeshi movement in Bengal and worked with revolutionaries such as Sri Aurobindo. But Upadhyaya did not renounce Hinduism, rather he continued to be a Hindu Catholic. Upadhyaya was the first to use the name *Satchidananda* for the 'Christian idea of Trinity within Christian church' (Thomas 1970: 102). Upadhyaya used Vedanta to understand Christian theology but here used the Thomist framework, not the mystical framework of Swami Vivekananda. Upadhyaya established an Ashram and introduced worship of Sarasvati – the Goddess of Learning – in his Ashram. About his journey as a Catholic Hindu he wrote: 'By birth we are Hindus and shall remain Hindu till death. But as *Dvija* [twice born] by virtue of our sacramental rebirth, we are catholics' (quoted in Thomas 1970: 109).

Pandita Ramabai (1858–1922) is another exemplary seeker who refused easy categorization and denominational fixation. She was a great wanderer, a courageous rebel and a creative being. She was born in a Brahmin family and had travelled with her parents the nook and corner of this country on foot. Ramabai was a critic of patriarchal Hinduism. When she accepted baptism while Brahmin reformers such as Ranade criticized her, Jyotirao Phule welcomed it and supported her (cf. Kosambi 2000; Omvedt 2008). Ramabai established a woman's home for widow and destitute called *Mutkisadan* (abode of liberation) in Khedgaon near Pune. Here she taught women how to live independently learning different trades, skills and vocations of life. Ramabai learnt Hebrew and translated Bible into Marathi. This was more creative and communicative compared to earlier missionary translation which was heavily Sanskritic.[33]

Ramabai lectured in the US about the same time as Swami Vivekananda was lecturing. She told her audience about the plight of high caste Hindu women and came into confrontation with Swami Vivekananda about missing this aspect of Hinduism in his representation of Hinduism to the West. But with her self-critical interrogation of her own Brahminical tradition, she was not an uncritical convert to the other side as well. As Schouten writes: 'While defending the Christian faith to Indian readers, she attempted to give English readers a better understanding of India's high civilization. [...] Like Rammohan Roy, she objected to the designation 'heathen' for a Hindu' (2012: 74).[34]

Sadhu Sundar Singh (1889–1929) was a convert to Christianity from the Sikh path and like Ramabai was not comfortable with denominational fixation. He lived the life of a wondering monk moving in between India and Tibet and like Ramabai also travelled around the world (Andrews 1934 quoted in Visvanathan 2007: 63). He was committed to an indigenous church in India: 'The water of life has hitherto been offered by thirsting souls in a European vessel. Only when it is given in an Eastern bowl will it be accepted by simple men and women who seek the truth' (ibid.: 86–87).

C.F. Andrews (1871–1940) came to India as an Anglican priest and soon immersed himself with freedom struggle of India as well as in the struggle for dignity on the part of the indentured Indians in Fiji, South Africa and around the world. He taught at St. Stephens and Tagore's Santiniketan (see Chaturvedi and Sykes 1949).[35] Bede Griffiths and Swami Abishiktananda (original name Henri Le Saux) also realized the spiritual paths in Hinduism and made deep dialogues with Vedanta and other streams of seeking realizations. Henri Le Saux, later known as Swami Abishiktananda (1910–1973), a Benedictine priest from France, came to India in 1949. In 1950, together with Fr Monchanin, who had come a decade earlier, he founded an Ashram near Trichy named Shantivanam. He was deeply influenced by Ramana Maharshi and also lived in a cave in Thiruvanmalai for sometime. For Ramana, 'the *guhantara*, the cave of the heart, the interior space of experience resolved all dualism, and it is this imagery that is the central symbol in Abishiktananda's writing' (Visvanathan 2007: 163). About his experience of Advaita, Swami Abishiktananda writes: 'The most terrifying experience for the Christian who experience Advaita is that the Lord himself goes away – it appears to tear him away from the Church and the sacraments which bind him to Christ' (quoted in Visvanathan 2007: 174).[36] He also writes:

> The more I live in India, and the more I am in touch with Hindus, the more certain I am that only spiritual means will transmit the message of the Gospel. The church was poor and a pariah under the Roman Empire during the first three centuries, but she was victorious. Here, in four centuries with money, good works, protection and [colonial] power and a host of missionaries, we have barely scratched the surface of India (ibid.: 181).[37]

Bede Griffiths known as Swami Dayananda also had a deep appreciation for the spiritual life of India: 'The first thing that I have learned is a simplicity of life which before I would have not thought possible. India has a way of reducing human needs to a minimum' (Griffiths 1976: 1; also see Griffiths 2003). He began with Kurusimala Ashram in Vagamon, Kerala and then moved to Shantivanam and breathed his last there.[38] Griffiths challenges us to realize the mystical dimension of Christianity and here he finds affinity between Sankara and Aquinas: 'Sankara and Aquinas were both mystics who had experienced the reality of the world which transcends the senses and could bring their intelligence to bear on that' (ibid.: 105). Griffiths finds yoga a spiritual way for the Christians as well finding similarity between the integral yoga of Sri Aurobindo and Christian yoga.[39]

The creative border-crossing and spiritual quest of Abishiktananda and Griffiths find a resonance in many Christians from India. They both belonged to the Christian Ashram movement of India though not totally closed within a view of Ashram as an institution. For them, sanyasa was a field of convergence between Hinduism and Christianity.[40] It must be noted that there is a long tradition of Ashram movement in India nurtured by such pioneering initiatives such as the Christa Prema Seva Ashram in Sivajinagar, Maharashtra, founded in 1927 by Anglican John 'Jack' Winslow.[41] In this field, along with Santivanam, Karisumala Ashram in Kerala is another whose founder Fr. Francis Acharya (originally known as Fr. Francis Mahieu, a Cistercian monk from Belgium) had stayed in Shantivanam in his early days as he had also drawn inspiration from Gandhi, especially Gandhi's concept of bread labour.[42] Sameeksha Center for Indian Spirituality based in Kalady, the birth place of Shankar, is another which works with inter-religious dialogue. It also pleads for creative border-crossing between Hinduism and Christianity. Sebastian Painadath from Sameeksha, as in one of the opening paragraphs of this essay, urges us to realize how Christians and Hindus can simultaneously realize the prophetic and mystical dimension in their social, religious and spiritual lives. Realizing the mystical dimension would help Christianity go beyond its exclusivism and realizing the prophetic dimension would help Hinduism to go beyond oppressive structures of many kinds such as caste system and realize self and social liberation.

Michael Amaladoss and Subhash Anand also bring deep realization to this journey of Hindu–Christian mutual co-realization. In his essay, 'From syncretism to Harmony', Michael Amaladoss tells us about his own journey as a Hindu Christian:

> We can think of another standpoint from within. For me, an Indian Christian, Hinduism is not an 'other' religion, as it is a foreign missionary. It is the religion of my ancestors. God has spoken to my ancestors through it. It is part of my tradition. I have my roots in it. I could say that I have two roots: Hinduism and Christianity. I will not find myself till I can discover and integrate the riches and human creativity – both these traditions have given to me. I am not anymore looking at Hindu scriptures, symbols and rituals from the outside as 'other,' but from within as 'mine.' Obviously I cannot have my feet in two boats at the same time. I will have to find a personal integration. Being a Christian, my integration of other religious elements will be around my experience of Jesus. I do not have to reject the Christian historical tradition but I will have to see that the Christian and Hindu traditions interact within me and my community in a creative manner. I will then be not only an 'Indian Christian,' but a 'Hindu-Christian,' my main identity being Christian. What I say here about Hinduism in my own personal case can be applied by others to Buddhism, Islam, Tribal, Dalits or other religions depending upon where their roots are (2008: 145).

Subhash Anand also embodies inspiring openness in his participation with some of the rivers of Hinduism. He applies the Upanishadic principle of *Bandhu* which means friendship to realize a more creative inter-relationship between Hindus and Christians theologically and practically. He tells us that when he is in a chapel he realizes Natraj as the Lord of Dance and also Christ as Dance.[43] He presents Natraj as a holistic Christian icon: 'Indeed, Jesus is the Dance of God, nay he is also the Lord of Dance' (2004: 167). Anand urges us to realize that Siva is not only male but also female, Siva is a womb which can also challenge us to realize Jesus as a mother, as a womb.[44]

Franics X. Clooney (2010) has explored some of the similarities between feminine spirituality in Hinduism and Christianity as part of a project of cross-cultural theology. But Clooney shares with us with inspiring honesty the difficulty of radically crossing one's identity as a Christian which, a journey we find in Griffiths and Abhishiktananda. Similarly, Felix Wilfred also challenges Christian theology and practice for more radical opening to Hinduism. Wilfred pleads for a Christian relativism as part of going beyond exclusive claims to truth. He also urges Christian institutions to go beyond their closed organizational logic and be part of wider democratic civil society of accountability, transparency and equal participation (Wilfred 2000). Wilfred challenges for a radical border-crossing in his *Margins: Site of Asian Theologies*:

> Reading the New Testament will reveal how it has all the things necessary for salvation. But I have been struck by the lack of one thing in the New Testament: the humour. Though the gospels are meant to convey joy and peace, yet humour does not seem to have a due place. A reading of the divine intervention in human history as through the avatar of Sri Krishna would bring in the element of play, both in God and also in human life. This play, in reality, is not expression of any frivolity. Through the play (*lila*) of Krishna is expressed the *unbound freedom of God and God's creation*. In fact creation is viewed as the play of God. What is happening at the microcosmic level with the play of Krishna is in fact the mirror of the macrocosmic reality of infinite freedom. [...] The magnetic pull of the milkmaids towards Krishna playing flute is nothing but the irresistible way the Divine power draws everything to itself. In Christian tradition we speak of the way the cross as the power of God's mystery draws us all [...] In short, a reading of the New Testament symbolism of the cross through the story of Krishna playing flute could be very enriching for both the traditions. A cross-scriptural reading of the New Testament message of the cross with the play and

aesthetics (*rasa*) involved in the play of flute by Krishna could save us also from the possible danger of masochistic trends (2008: 182).[45]

Interrogating Available Tropes of Hindu–Christian Engagement: Dalits and Adivasis

Hindus are not homogeneous. Scheduled castes who are now called Dalits constitute a major part of Hindu society. Dalits oppose Brahminical Hinduism and they as well as Dalit Christians in particular interrogate the terms such as Hindu Christians or Catholic Christians. For them this is the language and realization offered by what Frynkenberg (2010) calls 'trophies of grace', the high caste Hindu converts to Christianity who were preoccupied with mystical and other philosophical issues such as the significance of Vedanta in interpreting Christian Trinity.[46] They did not experience the pangs of social discrimination and their individual conversion did not alter the group humiliation of Dalits. Dalit Christians have interrogated the caste-ridden Christian church as well Hindu society. In Tamil Nadu, there is a vibrant movement of Dalit Christians which question casteist church practice as well as the wider social practice of caste domination and exclusion both theoretically and practically.[47] As David Mosse (2010) tells us, the priests from Dalit background question the caste bias of mainstream churches and they question the paternalism of the churches.[48]

While other Scheduled Castes and Dalits get benefit of reservations, Dalit Christians are not entitled to it. There is now a long struggle to reverse this decision. But in the mean time, many Dalit Christians in the Government schools use Hindu names to be able to avail of reservation benefits (Kumar and Robinson 2010).

Dalit Christians assert their own theology. According to Prasanna Kumari, Luther's theology of cross is most suited to the Dalit condition with their suffering (cf. Meshak 2007). A. Arul Maria Raj also talks about subversive Dalit theology and spirituality. For Sathianathan Clarke (1998), Dalits use drums in their day to day life. Dalit theology and spirituality is a theology and spirituality of drums – of beating drums against oppression and for liberation. For Clarke, '[...] the drum represents the Christic presence among the Dalits. [...] the drum depicts the 'No' of the Paraiyar to the colonizing and demonizing tendencies of the valuational system of caste communities. [...] The way of the suffering and path of Christ are intimately bound up in the drum' (1998: 188, 192, 194; also see Clarke et al. 2010).

Dalit Christians here not only build on symbols of their own life worlds such as drum and the available Christian theological resources such as the Lutheran theology of cross. They also build on centuries of *Nirguna* and critical spirituality cultivated by seekers and challengers such as Ravidas and Kabir (Robinson 2003). For example, in an ethnographic work on a Dalit from Uttar Pradesh named Massih, Mathew Schmalz tells about the continued significance of the Kabir tradition for the Dalits as well as Dalit Christians. John Massih joined a Christian Ashram of inculturation and found that in this place, there was no dialogue with the traditions of Kabir and Ravidas: 'Certainly, Kabir and Ravidas were as Indian as Patanjali or Shankara. But one did not hear their name mentioned in the ashram, either in morning meditation or in Indian Christian experience' (Schmalz 2010: 200).[49] Massih wrote a poem expressing his marginalization: 'How can one continue the struggle when one crosses over his life that lies before him, like a broken mirror [...] Oh, but I am a tiger in cage.'[50]

Christianity has also spread among the tribals of India who are called Adivasis through many processes including conversion which has been a subject of ire by many Hindus. But on the part of tribals, there is also an emergent move towards indigenization. Christian conversion has completely changed the religious affiliation of tribals in places like Nagaland. But there is also a yearning for roots here which is similar to that demonstrated in the longing of a Keshab Chandra Sen, a Pandita Ramabai or a Upadhyaya or a Amaladoss. A Christian leader from Nagaland tells us:

> […] I, like my Nagas, am a Christian, but I am not a European. I have a relationship with my God. Now my God can speak to me in dreams, just as happened to my Anglican ancestors. I do not have to be like Anglicans or Catholics and go through all those rituals. I do not need them. What I am talking about is Naga Christianity – an indigenous Naga Christianity (quoted in Frynkenberg 2010: 443).

We see the move towards indigenous Christianity among the tribals which is also part of an emergent tribal theology (see Lalruatkima 2010). This revival is part of a wider tribal awakening which we see in movements such as Danyi Polo in Arunachal Pradesh. But Lancy Lobo tells us about this complex process: '[…] through the process of indigenization the Catholic church seeks today to enmesh itself with the culture of its different community of believers. It is possible to be Christian and Adivasi […] On the other hand, there are processes at work within the Catholic church itself that might keep elite thinking and control effective in place' (Lobo 2010: 231).[51]

So movement towards Christianity in terms of conversion or the self-reflective moves of Christians and Christian communities have been accompanied by movements of indigenization and enculturation. While earlier these were thought of in terms of high-caste, Sanskritic and frames of reference such as Vedanta. Now these have been much more broadened involving multiple dialogues with histories, streams of alternative spirituality such as Kabir's, Dalit and Adivasi spirituality.[52]

Such moves have also led to creative efforts in literature, art and paintings. Here the works of Jyoti Sahi and Susheila Williams are inspiring. Sahi painted many pictures of Jesus embodying deeper cross-cultural spiritual realizations. Williams's picture 'The Man on a Village Tree' shows Jesus crucified in a tree.[53]

Hindu–Christian Engagement: Colonialism, Evangelism and Conversion

Hindu–Christian engagement took a complex turn with the coming of British colonial power in India. East Indian company did not encourage missionaries and the first European missionaries settled in areas other than ruled by the company such as the Danes. But slowly the situation changed and Christianity was seen by the local population as a ruling power. Missionaries and evangelists worked for conversion. They denigrated Hindu religion which created unease among the Hindus. But they also challenged practices such as caste which led to reform. Many Hindu organizations such as Ramakrishna Mission and Arya Samaj modeled their social service work to Christian social service institutions such as schools and hospitals.[54] While the Raj did not necessarily support the missionaries which Frynkenberg calls Hindu Raj, members of groups such as Bibhuti Sangha in Madras opposed Christian missionaries and attacked the converts. But despite this in many parts of India conversion from marginalized section of society went on. In places like South Travancore, London Missionary Society played an important role in this. Dick Kooiman's (1989) study of it shows us how the missionary work of LMS presented a way out for low-castes such as Shanars who later on came to be known as Nadars. With the inspiration from the missionaries Shanars protested against the dress code of the prevailing caste-ridden society such as Shanar women not allowed to wear upper garment (also see Gnanadason 1994).

But in terms of cultural interaction that the work of missionaries created Kooiman presents us an interesting picture. Caste Hindus came to hear the lectures of Samuel Mateir, a pioneer of the indigenization of church who transferred administrative responsibility to local people and ordained many locals as ministers. But the caste Hindus were not interested in conversion. While the low-caste converted and supported the work of his mission, they were not interested in scripture nor in the content of the belief. They were interested in material gains to their own condition of life.[55] But their primacy on material benefit has been many a time used as a judgmental stick to beat their act of conversion. Here Felix Wilfred (2012) challenges us to go beyond such a dualistic anthropology and spirituality. Wilfred asks: why conversion for the sake of spiritual illumination is necessarily superior to what is done for the realization of one's survival. Wilfred here challenges us to critically think beyond judgmental categories such as rice Christians, i.e. those Christians who converted for the sake of getting rice for their belly.[56] For Wilfred and other liberation theologians such as Walter Fernandez, conversion is not 'an encounter between Hinduism and Christianity, but a protest on the part of Dalits against social injustice' (Kim 2012: 203).

But coming to our historical story of conversion in South Travancore, it must be noted that here not all marginalized groups converted to Christianity. While Shanars converted, Iravazas found a way in the reform movement of Narayana Guru.[57] In South Travancore also there emerged a religious reformer named Muttukuti who presented himself as an incarnation of Vishnu and offered to the untouchable castes alternative pathways of recognition and dignity (cf. Patrick 2003). He inspired a movement known as Aya Vali which gave 'the subordinated Canars a realm of self-assertion, autonomy and agency, denied to them in the public sphere and in the economic and political realm' (ibid.: vii). But 'even as one section of society acknowledged Muttukuti as their religious leader, the missionaries of London Missionary Society, both of foreign and local origin, perceived him to be a threat to their missionary enterprises. They characterized him as Satan' (Patrick 2003: 84).

Missionary work and conversion created ripples in the existing society. It also led to new creativity as well as new ways of justifying old caste practice. For example, in Tamilnadu, H.A. Krishna Pillai (1827–1900) published *Rakshany Yatrikam* which was a Tamil adaptation of *Pilgrim's Progress*. It was 'the work of a lifetime. In over 4,000 verses, it expressed depths of Christian thought and feeling within the classical idiom of the ancient Sangam poets' (Frynkenberg 2010: 225).[58] For Dennis Hudson, his poetry shows both 'the continuity with the past in terms of a shared mystical vocabulary between Shrivaishnavism and Christianity, and the rupture that Krishna Pillai elaborates through his verse, when he describes, as he believes the delusions of his former religious life and the clarity of the Christian *marga* [...]' (quoted in Visvanathan 1993: 14). But Krishna Pillai's brother Muttaiya Pillai wrote a 'forceful treatise on the nature of difference and why symbols of difference were important to maintain' (ibid.).

Hindu–Christian Engagement: Continued and Contemporary Challenges

Colonialism, evangelism and conversion are critical questions which are not just confined to the past. For a long time, Hindus have been uneasy with the forces of conversion. Critics of forceful and fraudulent conversion includes Gandhi as well as forces of Hindu extremist organizations such as Rastriya Swayam Sevak and Bajrang Dal (Shourie 1994). But for this, it is not correct to group all these critics together (see Nadkarni 2003; 2008). Many Hindus feel offended the way their religions are portrayed by the missionaries and evangelists and would like to contribute to a transformation of such conditions of humiliation and disrespect. Some of these forces have now become more powerful and aggressive. For example, groups such as Jehova's Witnesses and the Pentecostals openly preach that their religion is the best and conversion is the only route left for non-Christians for realizing salvation.

In post-independent India there have been several legislations to address such concerns as well as to stop forcible and gullible conversion (see Mehta 2011). But these legislative moves are not innocent; they are enmeshed in wider politics of group identity, fear as well as the will to dominate. With all these difficulties, in the last quarter century Hindu extremist forces have targeted Christians and Christian communities in places like Gujarat and Odisha. The attack against Christians in Dang in the 1990s, the cruel and barbaric burning of Graham Staines and his two little sons Philip and Timothy, the murder of Swami Lakshmananda Saraswati in 2008 and the ensuring anti-Christian riots and violence is a cruel reminder of the persisting tension and violence in the relations between Hindus and Christians (cf. Giri 2005; 2009).

The Multiverse of Hindu-Christian Relations: Limits and Possibilities

In this journey, we have touched several aspects and dimensions of Hindu–Christian relations – historical, sociological, theological, spiritual, and ontological. Hindus and Christians have interacted with each other in complex fields of power, belief as well as quest for truth and self-realization. In this complex field, participants have interacted with each other not only as Hindu and Christians but have sought to realize themselves as seeking selves. In this seeking we find an ontological dimension of Hindu–Christian engagement which is not confined to ontology as essence or group identity but embodies a seeking self in quest for unbounded realization. This is a weak and practical ontology of vulnerability, love and labour (cf. Vattimo 1999; Dallmayr 2005). We find glimpses of this quest in Jesus himself as well as in Sri Ramakrishna, Vivekananda, Deepak Chopra, Chittaranjan Das, Bede Griffiths, Swami Abishiktananda, Felix Wilfred, Subhash Anand, Michael Amaladoss and Sebastian Painadath. These selves have also created ripples in group relations and the future of Hindu–Christian engagement depends upon further creative quest at the level of self and society.

This then brings us to the much talked about issue of the historical and the mystical.[59] Indian seekers in this multiverse of engagement such as Swami Vivekananda, Gandhi and Chittaranjan Das have not been dismissive of their responsibility to history but they have realized the limits of the historical and the significance of mystical in the direction of practical mysticism which includes cultivation of both the transcendental and immanent, material and spiritual, self as well as group. It seems further cultivation of practical mysticism going beyond the limits of dualism of history and mysticism and cultivation of simultaneous prophetic-mystical streams in both Hinduism and Christianity is a way out of the continued legacy of violence and lack of respect which still poisons part of our fields of life and society in India, Asia and the world.[60]

Note: I am grateful to Professor Ishwar Modi for his kind invitation to contribute to this special issue. I am in debt to Professors Felix Wilfred and Francis Clooney for their advice and help with this work.

Notes

1. Though there are controversies about it, Yogananda (2007) in his book refers to archival work and documentary evidence about it.
2. As Wilfred (2010: 217) writes:

   When Ram Mohan Roy, the Father of Indian Renaissance, wrote a little book on 'The Precept of Jesus', he was attempting to read universal ethics in the life and teachings of ethics in the Gospels was the beginning of a Hindu appraisal of Christianity in modern times. [...] But then sadly, instead of welcoming his effort to relate Jesus, the moral teacher, with Indian situation, his approach was resisted by missionaries because it did not tally with what they thought was the Christian belief system. [...] *A meaningful presence of Christianity in Asia seems to lie in what it could offer in terms of ethics than in terms of beliefs* (emphasis added).
3. It is to be noted that on 6 March 1881 Keshab celebrated 'the Blessed Sacrament with rice and water instead of bread and wine [...]' (Rolland 1954: 132).
4. Omvedt talks about the elitist character of Roy: '[Roy's arguments] were focused on the elite. [...] In fact, in presenting a religion of rationality and anti-idolatry monotheism, he was increasing the differentiation of the bhadralok from the subaltern masses – who were Vaishnavite devotee of one or another sect, who were not troubled by the problems of widow remarriage and sati but were very much troubled by caste. And caste was an issue that did not enter the agenda of the 'Renaissance' elite reformers' (2008: 148). But Keshab 'introduced Chaitanya into Brahmo religious practice' (Thomas 1970: 31).
5. Note here what Rolland writes about Keshab:

   A hyper-individualist by nature and doubtless just because this was the case, he early in his life recognized that part of evils of his country arose out of this same hyper-individualism, and that India needed to acquire a new moral conscience. 'Let all souls be socialized and realized their unity with the people, the visible community'. The conception uniting the aristocratic unitarianism of Roy to the Indian masses put young Keshab into communion with the most ardent aspirations of the rising generation. Just as Vivekananda in after days [...], Vivekananda believed religion to be necessary for the regeneration of race (1954: 118–19).

6. According to his biographer Arun Kumar Mukherjee, 'Keshab developed a new style of Bengali prose – forceful, fluent, simple and communicative. [... He also] developed a new style of English prose – based on oratory. It was poetical oratory which married itself to his highly spiritual teaching as perfect music unto noble minds' (1992: 59).
7. However, Thomas makes clear that Sen's project of Christ-centred integration was different from building a 'universal religion based on the equality of all religions' (1970: 73).
8. Though Rajiv Malhotra (2007) questions the equation of Spirit with Sakti, what Bede Griffiths (1976: 129) writes below resonates with many Hindus:

   The Spirit is the *Sakti* – the power – of the Godhead, the breath by which the Word is uttered, the energy which flows from the Father into the Word and overflows in the creation. It is by the Spirit that 'ideas' in the Word are given form and substance and the creation comes into being. [...] The Spirit is the feminine principle in the Godhead, the Mother of all creation. It is in her that the seeds of the Word are planted and she nurtures them and brings them forth in creation. [...] It is the Spirit which is continually drawing us into the divine life. For the Spirit is that divine life latent in nature and becoming conscious in us. By the Spirit we know that we are not merely flesh and blood, formed from the matter of the universe, not merely the subject of sensations, feelings, imaginations and thoughts, but an energy of love which seeks always to transcend the barriers of space and time and to discover the Divine Life.

   The above meditation and realization of Spirit as Sakti can be an invitation to Christians especially Pentecostals who speak a lot about the Spirit. But while their Spirit seems to be mainly confined to gift of Tongues, Griffiths' cross-cultural and spiritual realization of Spirit can be a transformative stream in contemporary Christianity not only in Asia but all over the world.
9. Ramakrishna's biographer Romain Rolland writes about it:

   Sometimes around November 1874, a certain Mallik, a Hindu of Calcutta, with a garden near Dakhineswar read the Bible to him. For the first time Ramakrishna met Christ. Shortly afterwards

> the word was made flesh. The life of Jesus secretly pervaded him. One day when he was sitting in the room of a friend, a rich Hindu, he saw on the wall a picture representing the Madonna and the Child. The figures became alive. Then the expected came to pass according to the invariable order of the Spirit; the holy visions came close to him and entered into him so that his whole being was being impregnated with them. Then one afternoon in the grave of Dakhineswar he saw coming towards him a person with beautiful large eyes, a serene regond and a fair skin. Although he did not know who it was, he succumbed to the charm of his unknown guest. He drew near and a voice sang in the depths of Ramakrishna's soul: Behold the Christ, who shed his heart's blood for the redemption of the world, who suffered a sea of anguish for love of men. It is He, the master Yogin, who is in eternal union with God. It is Jesus, Love incarnate. [...] The son of Man embraced the son of the Mother, and became merged in him. Ramakrishna was lost in ecstasy. Once again he realized union with Brahman. Then gradually he came down to earth, but from that time he believed in the Divinity of Jesus Christ, the Incarnate God. But for him Christ was not the only Incarnation. Buddha and Krishna were others in India (1954: 83, 87).

10. In his address Swami Vivekananda challenged his audience:

> With all your attempts to paint him with blue eyes and yellow hair, the Nazarene was still an Oriental. All the similes, the imageries, in which the Bible is written – the scenes, the locations, the attitudes, the groups, the poetry and symbol – speak to you of the Orient, of the bright sky, of the heat, of the sun, of the desert, of the thirsty men and animals; of men and women coming with pitchers on their heads to fill them at wells; of the flocks, of the ploughmen, of the cultivation that is going on around; of the water-mill and wheel, of the mill-pond, of the millstones. All these are to be seen today in Asia (2011: 11–12).

11. For Swami Vivekananda,

> We are not here to discuss how much of the New Testament is true, we are not here to discuss how much of that life is historical. [...] But there is something behind it, something we want to imitate. [...] You cannot imitate that which you never perceived. But there must have been a nucleus, a tremendous power that came down, a marvelous manifestation of spiritual power – and of that we are speaking (2011: 22–23).

12. Thomas does this when he writes:

> Vivekananda rejects the ethical Christ for the mystic Christ [...] the Sermon on the Mount, for Vivekananda, is not primarily ethics, but an expression of the spirituality of self-renunciation (1970: 125).

13. Chittaranjan Das used to often tell us about this story (see Das 1995). Romain Rolland also makes an interesting remark that without this continuous challenge from Sri Ramakrishna, Swami Vivekananda would have become another Dayananda Sarasvati: 'Dayananda was what Vivekananda would have been, if he had not encountered Ramakrishna' (1954: 143). Both Swami Dayananda and Swami Vivekananda had enormous energy but Rolland suggests that it is Ramakrishna's influence which made the later socially committed to transforming suffering as well as open to other religions such as Christianity. While Swami Dayananda Sarasvati was also engaged with social upliftment, he lacked Ramakrishna-Vivekananda dialogical engagement with other religions.
14. About this it is written in one of the records of Ramakrishna Mission:

> The story begins on a winter night in a village named Antpur not very far from Calcutta. Some young monks were gathered around a blazing fire under the open sky. They were all direct disciples of Ramakrishna. [...] That night, after a long session of meditation, Narendranath told his *gurubhais* the story of Jesus Christ, the mystery of His wondrous birth and death and His subsequent resurrection. Through the eloquence of Narendra, the boys were admitted to the apostolic world where in Paul had preached the Gospel of the arisen Christ and Naren made his plea to them to become Christs themselves to realize God [...] standing before *dhuni* (wood-fire), with the flames lighting up their countenances and cracking of the wood as the sole disturbance of their thoughts, they took the vow of Sannyasa before God and one another (Vivekananda Kendra Prakashan Trust 2009: 9–10).

Romain Rolland also writes about the initial period of the seminary and the mission:

> In this panorama of all the heroic and divine thoughts of humanity, we must again notice the place of honour which seems to have been given to Christ and the Gospels. These Hindu monks kept Good Friday, and they sang the Canticles of St Francis. Naren spoke to them of Christian saints, the founders of the Western Orders. The Imitation of Jesus Christ was their

> bedside book together with the Bhagavad-Gita. Nevertheless there was never for a moment any question of enrolling themselves with the Church of Christ. They were and remained complete and uncompromising Vedantic Advaitists. But they incorporated in their faith all the faiths of the world. The waters of the Jordan mingled with their Ganga (2010: 8).

15. As Chakkarai tells us: '[...] the mere Scripture teaching would not have any impression on my mind and lately by the advent of Swami, whose conception of the catholicity of Vedanta destroyed my Hindu prejudices against Christianity as a foreign religion. It was he who first taught me to regard Christianity as an essentially Oriental faith' (quoted in Pandian 2010: 34).
16. Schouten further tells us:

> Ranganathananda quotes two texts from the Upanishads in order to demonstrate that the goal in both religions is identical. These texts could be translated as 'Verily, the self must be seen' and 'He who is without desire, sees the greatness of the self' (Brihad-Aranyaka Upanishad 11: 45; Katha Upanishad 1: 2: 20). Typical for the linguistic usage in the Ramakrishna Movement is that in both texts the words for 'see' are translated by 'realize'. All emphasis is on deliberate human endeavour (2012: 100).

17. In this context, what Thomas writes below deserves our careful consideration:

> While Brahmoism as a movement of reform in Hinduism had absorbed a great many of the Christian notions about religion it had very shallow roots in the fundamental metaphysical framework of Hinduism. Nehemiah Goreh was certainly right in asserting that this metaphysical framework was Advaita Vedanta [...] and, as he predicted, Brahmoism withered, without roots either in fundamental Hinduism or in Christian revelation. But what he did not predict did happen, namely, the redefinition of Advaita Vedanta, with its assertion of its mystic centre, but with a capacity to absorb into its framework the value of moral struggle and social service (1970: 146).

18. Paramahansa Yogananda writes:

> We must know Jesus as Oriental Christ, a supreme Yogi who manifested full mastery of the universal science of God-Union, and thus could speak, and act as a Saviour with the voice and authority of God. He has been Westernized too much (2007: 90).

19. In the words of Radhakrishnan:

> The abandonment of the ego is the identification with a fuller life and consciousness. The soul is raised to a sense of its

universality. In Gethsemane, Christ as an individual felt that the ego should pass away. […] The secret of the cross is the crucifixion of the ego and the yielding to the will of God. 'Thy will be done' (quoted in Thomas 1970: 100).

In a recent essay, Jesudas Athyal also tells us that Radhakrishnan in his *Eastern Religions and Western Thought* attempts to 'demonstrate inter alia that Christ and Christianity were influenced by many Eastern elements such as mysticism, asceticism and non-violence' (2012: 578).

20. Speaking of his experience of being with Gandhi at his historic fast in Delhi, C.F. Andrews writes:

    Instinctively my gaze turned back to the frail, wasted, tortured spirit on the terrace by my side, bearing the sins and sorrows of his people. […] And in that hour of vision, I knew more deeply, in my own personal life, the meaning of the Cross (quoted in Thomas 1970: 226).

21. George lived with his conviction:

    An undogmatic Christianity, true to the spiritual insight of Jesus of Nazareth, will yet discover and establish its links with liberal elements in all other religions, and will especially find its rightful place in that larger fellowship of faiths that is yet to be (quoted in Thomas 1970: 219).

22. Here John Mary's work sheds much light. He tells us about one 'Joseph Baptista (1864–1930), fondly called Kaka Baptista, [who] was a close friend of Bala Gangadhara Tilak. He is claimed to be the one who first suggested the Home Rule Movement to Tilak even before Annie Besant launched it' (2011: 61).

23. For George, '[…] Unlike a natural phenomenon a spiritual fact is a challenge – you have got to do something about it – make up your mind, take an attitude towards it. […] Gandhi is a spiritual fact of this category' (1939: 23).

24. Radhakrishna also raises the issue of cross-cultural realization and understanding of Christianity in India in this foreword:

    If Europe interpreted Christianity in terms of his own culture, Greek thought and Roman imagination, there is no reason why Indian Christian should not relate the message of salvation in Christ to the larger spiritual background of India. Possibly, India's religious insight may help to revive Christianity, not only in India but the world at large. Can't we have a Vedanta tradition in Christianity? The late Max Muller thought of himself as a Christian Vedantin. There are thousands in the West today who have acquired a new and deeper impulse of

> religious life through the influence of Hindu thought. If even non-Indian Christian find it easier to understand Christianity in the light of Vedanta, it is unfortunate that Indian Christians are led to adopt an attitude of indifference, if not hostility, to Hindu religion and metaphysics (quoted in George 1939: 10).

25. Gandhi considered Jesus Christ a supreme artist because for him, Jesus lived life as a whole. He wanted to live life as a work of art as Jesus did and he wanted also to die like him. In his visit to Vatican in 1931 while looking at the pictures, he stood in silence and meditation in front of the picture of Crucifixion (from talk of Narayana Desai, 'Gandhi and the Arts', Kalakshetra Foundation, 8 September 2012).
26. It is probably for this reason that Sri Aurobindo had once commented that Gandhi's Christianity is Russian Christianity.
27. Though in his critique of missionary conversion Gandhi sometimes used a language of disrespect which needs transformation:

> Would you preach the Gospel to a cow? Well, some of the Untouchables are worse than cows in understanding. I mean they can no more distinguish between the relative merits of Islam, Hinduism and Christianity than a cow (quoted in Wilfred 2007: 146).

28. It is important here also to note the dialogue between Azariah and Ambedkar. Rudolf C. Heredia tells us about it:

> In 1936 Ambedkar met Azariah and asked, if in becoming Christians the Harijans would be united as one people in one church, free from prejudice, Azariah later admitted that he had never felt so ashamed because he could not answer 'yes', but could only come away in disgrace (2007: 71).

29. Schouten helps us understand the influence of his family background especially the devotional background of her mother belonging to the *Pranami sampradaya* on Gandhi's open-ended approach to religion:

> Gandhi's mother 'belonged to the *Pranami sampradaya*. [...] The more remarkable thing about this school in Vaishnavism is its extensive openness towards other religious traditions, both within and outside of Hinduism. This included a remarkable habit of placing various sacred texts next to one another to read and worship (2012: 150–51).

About Swami Prannath, the leader of this community, Schouten writes:

> Swami Prannath was the leader of the pranamis in the second half of the 17th century. [...] He was gradually convinced that all religions ultimately came down to the same thing. [...] To enlarge his knowledge of Islam, he made various trips to Arabic countries where he built up contacts with Islamic theologians. Nor did the Christian faith lie outside of his interest. Through the Portuguese and British people he encountered in the harbor city of Gujarat, he acquired some knowledge of the Bible and Church doctrine (2012: 152).

30. Das tells us about it:

    > In 1322, it is said, Pope John XXII condemned as heretical the doctrine of poverty of Christ and thereafter the early lives of St Francis were rewritten to down the unfortunate views of the founder on that subject (2012: 28).

31. Sri Aurobindo hints at it in his essay, 'Our Ideals' when he talks about Buddhism and Vaishnavism impacting Semitic temperament through Christianity. Yogananda (2007) also talks about the journey of Jesus to India and Tibet and he gives documentary evidence of it.
32. Harrison tells us that 'exemplary reasoning' is different from 'scriptural reasoning' and inter-religious dialogue through 'exemplary practitioners of one's faith' (2011: 24). Furthermore, 'exemplary reasoning is, essentially, a process of thinking with others about examples or models. The use of the term 'reasoning' rather than 'reason' indicates that it is involved in an ongoing process of reflection' (ibid.: 29).
33. Schouten writes about it:

    > [In earlier translation] The religious terminology was derived partly from Sanskrit and she suspected that elements of Hinduism came with them. [...] She studied Greek and also acquired some knowledge of Hebrew. Moreover, she made use of the linguistic skills of Indians of Jewish ancestry, from the 'Beni-Israeli community'. She completed her translation of the Bible shortly before her death in 1922 (2012: 72).

    Chittaranjan Das also writes the following about her translation: 'Ramabai's translation is in simple colloquial Marathi in a style very different from the archaic classical way in which the missionaries have done it' (2012: 235–36).

34. Robert Eric Frynkenberg (2010: 390) also tells us:

    > Ramabai continued to see herself as both 'Hindu' and 'Christian' – a pilgrim attempting to resolve inner conflicts within herself and within her own people in India. Refusing to become a clone, a proselyte, or a hostage of either Anglican, or any other form of

> Christendom, she withstood each onslaught and kept her balance. Within her lay a toughness forged on anvils of hard experience [...].

35. Once a missionary asked Gandhi, 'How do you think should the missionaries identify themselves with the masses? The answer was just three words: "Copy Charlie Andrews"' (quoted in Visvanathan 2007: 63).
36. For Swami Abishiktananda,

> Advaita is already present at the root of the Christian experience. It is simply the mystery that God and world are not two. The mystery of unity, ekatvam, in God and in all works of God, is personified by the Spirit. Before leaving his disciples, Jesus laid great stress on the mysterious presence of Spirit in them [...].
>
> Instead of speaking of synthesis or transcendence, it would be much more accurate to speak of the advaitic dimension of revelation and of Christianity. This is also a dimension inherent in the act of faith which leads to salvation – we should perhaps call it a dimension of depth, of which contact with the Upanishadic experience makes one more fully aware (1969: 101).

Furthermore,

> The problem which Advaita poses for the Church is in fact an existential one. It is a providential means of purification offered to the Church by God at the very moment when her encounter with the modern technological world of the West has made her more than ever aware of the burden of her history and her deep need for a return to her spiritual roots.
>
> Advaita does not however ask of Christianity that it should transcend itself, and set out towards a further goal beyond itself, any more than Christianity asks Vedanta to disown all that it is, in order to transcend itself and be transformed into Christianity. If there must be a transcendence, then what is needed is an inward transcendence. For both Christianity and Vedanta this means that they should continue to dig down ever more deeply in search of their own living sources, should investigate ever more profoundly the secret of their own being, until each discovers in the other the presence of its own most inward mystery (ibid.: 106).

He also challenges us to realize the comparative significance of Christian encounter with Greek and Upanishadic spirits:

> Greece was chosen for a different mission. She had to provide the infant church with the means of expressing its conceptual terms the essential message she had received from the Lord [...].
>
> To the Vedantic experience, however, was entrusted the task of preparing for the Spirit of Wisdom. Although in older times than the Greek discovery of the world of the intellect, it has been called later in history to make its contribution to the Church and so enter into the plan of salvation. This is fitting; for it opens up to the action of grace that level of the human psyche which seems to mark the culmination of all that man is capable of finding and realizing in himself. In the design of providence Vedanta is surely the ultimate preparation for the Gospel, for it opens to action of grace that level of the human psyche which seems to mark the culmination of all that man is capable of finding and realizing in himself. In the design of providence, Vedanta is surely the ultimate preparation for the Gospel, for it disposes man to comprehend its most sublime mysteries [...] (ibid.: 118).

37. He also writes: 'The Church of the poor ought to be, not a Church that gives to the poor, but one which lives in poverty' (quoted in Visvanathan 2007: 185).

38. Kurusimala Ashram is more liturgical in its prayer while in Santivanam the mode of prayer is more contemplative and open-ended. According to Jesu Rajan, 'His [Bede Griffith's] movement from Kurusimala 'Hill of the Cross' to Santivana 'Forest of Peace' is not a mere geographical movement. It is, rather a theological movement, a movement from a life centered on liturgy and community life to a life centered on contemplation' (1989: 216).

    Griffiths himself tells us about it:

    > We no longer see the liturgy of common prayer as the center of life of a monk. It is the contemplative prayer when Holy Spirit is experienced in its immediate presence and not through outward signs that becomes the center of the life of a monk. [...] If we make the liturgy and Eucharist the center of our lives we necessarily exclude Hindus and people of any other religion from our inner life. It is not in external rites, however sacred, that we make contrast with our brother and sisters in other religions but through mediation and contemplative prayer (quoted in Rajan 1989: 204).

39. What Griffiths writes deserves our careful consideration here:

    > In the integral yoga of Sri Aurobindo the values of matter and life and the human consciousness and the experience of

> personal God are not lost in the Ultimate Reality, the divine Sachhidananda. Matter and life and consciousness in man are seen to be evolving towards the divine life and divine consciousness, in which they are not annihilated but fulfilled.
>
> This is the goal of a Christian yoga. Body and soul are to be transfigured by the divine life and to participate in the divine consciousness (1976: 138).

40. For Bede Griffiths, 'true convergence between Hinduism and Christianity can take place mainly in the life of *Sannyasa*' (quoted in Rajan 1989: 149). What Rajan writes below about the vocation of a Christian sannyasin deserves our careful attention:

    > To a Christian *Sannyasin* Jesus is his *sadguru*, the true guru. [...] He leads him to the *Paramguru*, the Father. [...] Obedience of a Christian sannyasin could be compared to a jnana yoga. [...] Knowledge of the Supreme Reality, Brahmavidya, frees a person from all bondage. In the same way the Christian *sannyasin* who surrenders his self to the Supreme Reality finds true freedom [...] (ibid.: 210).

41. According to Paul Prathathu, 'Today there are more than hundred of Christian ashrams, both Catholic and Protestant, experimenting in community living, in rural service, in indigenous worship and in theological research in various branches through different *sadhanas*' (1997: 207).

    What Prathathu writes below about the spiritual theology of Ashram deserves our careful attention:

    > The ashram is a place of spiritual effort-srama. [...] Holiness in Wholeness is a unique contribution of the Christian ashram. Holiness is the goal of life at the Christian ashram. Integration is the principle of srama there. [...] The whole srama is oriented towards integration. It is an integration of the divine and the human with that of the Cosmic (ibid.: 271).

42. The Ashram which is located in a hill near Vagmanon, Kerala combines Indian spiritual practices such as meditation and singing of devotional songs with Christian spiritual practice especially from the Benedictian-Cisterian tradition. As the Ashram was inspired by Gandhi's concept of bread labour, here monks earn their livelihood by raising and milking cows. Gandhi himself was inspired by the Cisterian spiritual tradition. After a visit to a monastery in South Africa, Gandhi had written:

    > I once stayed with Cistercian monks. They are votaries of divine love, of poverty, of chastity. Their monastery was a veritable garden. There was a sweet silence pervading the whole

atmosphere. I still live under the charm of their cells. It would be my ideal to found such an institution.

43. Anand writes:

> Sometimes I sit for prayer in a chapel with darkness all around me. More than once I have caught myself contemplating the flame of the oil-lamp placed close to the tabernacle. The dance of the fire grips me, and I can go on watching it for long, unmindful of the passing of time. Slowly as I began to meditate on the Nataraj icon – and I have been doing this for quite some years now – I understand a little what was happening to me. The Spirit whom I received in Baptism has not pushed out the Spirit I received from my ancestors. The more I try to contemplate the Nataraj icon the more it fascinates me, and I thank God for making me a child of the land which has given to the world an icon which is aesthetically superb and theologically profound. This icon fascinates me all the more because I am trying to reflect on my Christian faith in the light of Hindu wisdom. I find the Nataraj icon very appropriate to express my own faith.
>
> Jesus tells us that God, who as the perfect Being (sat) grounds all being, is a most loving Father. He is indeed the Merciful One. He is Shiva. In Him there is perfect self-possession and self-awareness (cit): the primordial Word (*logos* or *sabda*). From this perfect self-awareness of perfect Being arises the perfect joy of Being (*ananda*), and from this springs forth Breath (pneuma) that Spirit which makes Speech (*vac*) possible. The Nataraj icon can be seen as expressive of this Trinitarian mystery (2004: 168–69).

Here the following thoughts of Henryk Skolimowski on dancing Shiva are helpful and we can read these together with Anand and realize the deeper significance of a dancing Shiva and dancing Christ in our lives, societies and the cosmos:

> Dancing Shiva is the symbol of life unfolding, of recreating itself, partly destroying itself in order to create *novo*. Dancing Shiva is you and me engaged in the creative/destructive process of life. [...] The eternal dance of Shiva becomes the dance of healing – of the planet and ourselves, becomes the dance of purifying our rivers, our mountains and our bodies. [...] The new dance of Shiva is a form of Eco-Yoga, for the whole society [...] (1991: 5, 10, 13).

44. Anand writes:

> Siva too has a maternal side deep within him because he is *ardha-nari-isvara*, and *lasya* is his tender, nurturing dance. It is very significant that, in the *Siva-Sahasra-nama*, Siva is

> described not only as the great male organ (maha-linga, 74a) – but only once, and also as the great womb (maha-garbha, 81d, 103c, 131a) – that too thrice! In primal symbolism the tree has a great affinity with woman and hence a maternal character. Siva not only appears like a tree, but himself the cosmic Tree (2004: 163).

I have also explored this in part of the following poem:

> Mata Krista Namoh, Krista Mata Nama
> Garva Krista Namoh, Christa Garbha Namoh
>
> (Salutations to Mother Christ, Christ Mother
> Salutations to Womb Christ, Christ Womb)

I have also explored Cross as our mother in the following poem, 'Cross! Our Mother':

> Oh Cross!
> Our Mother
> Your Four Sides
> The Crucified Middle
> Are Not Only a Square
> Of Torture, Suffering and Cruelty
> You are a Circle of Compassion
> Of One and Many –
> Nature, Divine and Man
> Of Meeting and Evolution
>
> Oh Cross!
> You are a Field
> In Your Field
> We learn our
> Limitations and Possibilities
> In your lap
> Hands of compassion
> Give us strength
> Trust and Hope
> We embrace you
> Our pain and suffering
> Become circles of awakening
> From ashes arise the Gold
> Flowers of Transformations

45. We can also here bring together Anand's realization of Christ as dancing Shiva and Wilfred's realization of Christ as flute playing Krishna.

46. In the words of Frynkenberg:

> Many of these Brahmin Christians focused their attention on intellectual or mystical-cum-spiritual (bhakti) issues [...] that

> sought for links between the great traditions from which they themselves had come and from which most of them never entirely parted. Even Pandita Ramabai's own *bhakti* devotionalism did not begin to veer away from her own pure [...] identity until after her third Christian conversion and the 'Holy Ghost' revival that broke twenty years later (1905) at the Mukti Mission in Kedagaon. Nor can the Christian career of Sadhu Sundar Singh be seen as reflecting a close identification with either *Adivasi* or *avarna* forms of Indian Christianity [...] (2010: 457).

47. Mosse writes about this:

> [...] A Dalit-focused caste-based approach to social activism gradually became the predominant form among activists within the priesthood, beginning with the Jesuits of Madurai Province, whose anti-caste 'social action ministry' inverted the social 'accommodations' of their 17th century founder Robert de Nobili. Indeed, from 1987 the Jesuit 'option for the poor' had been firmly recast as a Dalit option [... But] despite its 'Dalit option', only 18 of the 300 odd Jesuit priests were Dalits (2010: 237, 239).

48. For Mosse, '[...] as public service institutions, Catholic schools and technical colleges transacted symbols of caste honor and prestige much as temples or churches did in the past' (2010: 245).
49. Pandian (2010) offers a similar critique of Vengal Chakkarai's project of indigenization which for him is mainly Brahminical.
50. The following interpretation is insightful:

> Even in its brevity, the partial poem is replete with words evocative of Dalits and their condition: 'struggle' (*sangharsh*), 'cage' (*pinjara*) and 'tiger' (*sher*). But the image of the 'broken mirror' (*tuta darpan*) says the most about John, not to mention Dalit religion on the margins. In *nirguni* poetry, the mirror is often a sign of vanity, as it is in Kabir's famous song 'what face do you see in the mirror' (*darpana*)? In one sense, John uses the mirror to represent his reflecting on his shattered pride. In another sense, he also seems to be mourning his lost dreams (Schmalz 2010: 206).

51. In his study of Christianity among the Oraons, Peggy Froerer tells us how Christian church and the priests demonize the local deities and subject the practitioners to social and financial punishment: '[...] a system of ostracism and fines is instituted against those found guilty in Unchristian activities, with a mechanism of excommunication or 'outcasting', where participants are excluded from

the school until such fines are paid and confession is extracted' (2010: 135; also see Froerer 2007).

52. This is in tune with the perspectives of scholars such as Judith Brown and Robert Frynkenberg. For Brown, 'India's history has been marked by a religious pluralism in which converts to Christianity carried with them much from their former beliefs and cultural practices' (Coward 2004; cf. Brown and Frynkenberg 2002).This has contributed to 'new Indian modes of worship and theological emphasis' (ibid.).

53. For Schouten,

    Under the influence of *dalit* theology we see another representation of Jesus emerging in recent years. In addition to what has now become the traditional depiction of an exalted teacher of wisdom or a cosmic figure, we now see him in villages, associated with the culture of the low-caste people. Jyoti Sahi, for instance, painted Christ in his later work a dancer who impassions people with a large hand drum (2012: 255).

54. Rajeev Bhargava (2012) discusses some of these changes in Hindu organizations and the accompanying processes of what he calls 'social democratization' but he does not seem to acknowledge how these changes were brought about by encounter with Christianity.

55. Samuel Meteir, who spent the better part of his life among the *Pulayas* of Trivandrum district, summarized their frank enquiries about the temporal benefits of Christianity in the following way:

    What is the profit of learning your religion? Will you feed us? Shall we be freed from dying? Shall we be allowed to steal when we are hungry and have nothing to eat? May we take as many wives as we please? (quoted in Kooiman 1989: 170).

56. For Wilfred, such labeling reflects a 'dichotomous anthropology, which contrasts and hierarchizes the material and the spiritual in human. By hierarchizing the material and the spiritual, and subordinating the latter to the former a framework is created for the subordination of Dalits to the caste-Christians, who represent higher spiritual realm' (2012: 594). Wilfred also challenges us to understand the longing for material security on the part of the low-caste and the rich people's craving for money:

    The quest for rice was a quest for life, and it cannot be placed on par with the greed for material possessions by the rich and the powerful. [...] In their search for material goods, security and dignity in the church, our Dalit sisters and brothers were seeking life, which they continue to affirm with the power of the

Spirit against those who deny it through individual and collective selfishness (ibid.: 596).

The conflict between material and spiritual that Wilfred talks about finds an interesting resonance in the Webb Keane's (2007) study of conversion in Indonesia. For Keane while Dutch missionaries focused on content of belief, the people of Shumba were interested in their material objects which were denigrated as fetishes by the missionaries.

57. Shnaras now Nadars belonged to low-caste position in South Travancore while the Iravazas, also considered untouchable in caste hierarchy, belonged to North Travancore.

58. Felix Wilfred (personal communication) here urges us to understand the influence of Hindu tradition in the creation of Christian literature: 'For example, the widely acclaimed classic *Thembavani* by the Italian missionary Beschi reflects the way Hindu gods and goddesses are presented in traditional literature'.

59. Some Hindus here think that Judeo-Christian tradition is reluctant to give up its history-centeredness which would also make it give up its claim to uniqueness: 'Jewish and Christian religions cannot afford to compromise on their history-centric beliefs, because to do so would be tantamount to surrendering their claim of uniqueness access to knowledge of God's will' (Malhotra 2011: 90). For Rajiv Malhotra, here yoga provides freedom from history.

60. Here we can reflect upon the following conversation between Ramin Jahanbegloo and Peter Desouza in which Jahanbegloo asks De Souza: '[Vivekananda] entertained a vision of India having a Vedantic brain, an Islamic body, and a Christian heart. Do you think India today has a Christian heart?' (2008: 164). De Souza replies: 'I think if there is something like Christian heart then we would like to have it. I think the idea of fraternity, brotherhood and sisterhood is there in Christianity. The world is moving away from these sensibilities and that's the cause for some degree of gloom actually' (ibid.).

References

Abishiktananda, 1969, *Hindu-Christian Meeting*, ISPCK, Delhi.

——, 1975, *The Further Shore*, ISPCK, Delhi.

Amaladoss, Anand et al., 2005, *Preaching Wisdom to the Wise: Three Treatises by Roberto de Nobili, S.J. Missionary, Scholar and Saint in 17th Century India*, Satya Nilayam, Chennai.

Amaladoss, Michael S.J., 2008, *Beyond Dialogue: Pilgrims in the Absolute*, Asian Trading Corporation, Bangalore.

Anand, Subhash, 1994, *Story as Theology: An Interpretative Study of Five Episodes from the Mahabharata*, Intercultural Publications, New Delhi.

——, 2004, *Hindu Inspiration for Christian Reflections: Towards a Hindu-Christian Theology*, Gujarat Sahitya Prakashan, Anand.

Athyal, Jesudas, 2012, 'Non-Baptized Believers in Christ', *Hedlund.*

Bhargava, Rajeev, 2012, 'Hinduism and Social Democratization: A Preliminary Sketch', in Partha Chatterjee and Ira Katznelson (eds), *Anxiety of Democracy: Tocquevillian Reflections on India and the United States*, OUP, Delhi.

Brown, Judith M. and Robert E. Frynkenberg (eds) 2002, *Christians, Cultural Interactions and India's Religious Traditions*, Routledge-Curzon, London.

Chaturvedi, Benarasidas and Marjorie Sykes, 1949, *Charles Freer Andrews*, George Allen & Unwin, London.

Chopra, Deepak, 2008, *The Third Jesus: How to Find Truth and Love in Today's World*, Reider, London.

Clarke, Sathianathan, 1998, *Dalits and Christianity: Subaltern Religion and Liberation Theology in India*, OUP, Delhi.

Clarke, Sathianathan et al. (eds) 2010, *Dalit Theology in the Twenty-First Century: Discordant Voices, Discerning Pathways*, OUP, Delhi.

Das, Chittaranjan, 2012, 'Jesus Christ, White, Black or Yellow?', in *On the Side of Life In Spite of*, Sahitya Akademi, Delhi.

Dallmayr, Fred, 2005, *Small Wonder: Global Power and its Discontents*, Rowman & Littlefield, Lanham, MD.

Devasahayam, V. (ed.) 1996, *Frontiers of Dalit Theology*, Gurukul Summer Institute, Chennai.

Dhavamony, Mariasusai, 2009, *Hindu-Christian Dialogue: Theological Sounding and Perspectives*, Overseas Indian Press, Delhi.

Francis X. Clooney, S.J., 2010, *Comparative Theology: Deep Learning Across Religious Borders*, Wiley-Blackwell, Oxford.

Froerer, Peggy, 2007, *Religious Division and Social Conflict: The Emergence of Hindu Nationalism in Rural India*, Social Science Press, Delhi.

Frynkenberg, Robert E., 2010, *Christianity in India: From the Beginnings to the Present*, OUP, Oxford.

George, S.K., 1939, *Gandhi's Challenge to Christianity*, George Allen & Unwin Ltd., London.

Giri, Ananta Kumar, 2004, 'Love and Fire', in *Reflections and Mobilizations: Dialogues with Movements and Voluntary Organizations*, Sage, Delhi.

——, 2009, 'Peace in Kandhamal', *Mainstream*.

Gnanadason, Joy, 1994, *A Forgotten History: The Story of the Missionary Movement and the Liberation of People in South Travancore*, Gurukul Lutheran Theological College and Research Institute, Chennai.

Griffiths, Bede, 1976, *Return to the Center*, Fount Paperbacks, London.

——, 2003 [1976], *The Golden String: An Autobiography*, Media Publishers, Tucson, Arizona.

Haldar, Dipankar, nd, 'The Realisation of Kingdom of God in Neo-Vedanta', www.biblicalstores.org.uk, accessed on 27 January 2012.

Harrison, Victoria, 2011, 'Embodied Values and Muslim-Christian Dialogue: "Exemplary Reasoning" as a Model for Interreligious Conversations', *Studies in Interreligious Dialogue*, Vol. 21, No. 1.

Hancock, Mary E., 2010, 'Landscapes of Christianity in Colonial South India: The Matter of Hindu Ritual and Christian Conversion, 1870–1920'. In Michael Bergunder et al. (eds) *Ritual, Caste, and Religion in Colonial South India*, Halle: Verlag der Frankeschen Stiftungen.

Hedlund, Roger (eds), 2012, *Oxford Encyclopedia of South Asian Christianity*, OUP, Delhi.

Heredia, Rudolf C., 2007, *Changing Gods: Rethinking Conversion in India*, OUP, Delhi.

Jahanbegloo, Ramin, 2008, *India Revisited: Conversations on Contemporary India*, OUP, Delhi.

Jevtic, Miroljub, 2007, 'Political Science and Religion', *Politics and Religion Journal*, Vol. 1, No. 1.

——, 2008, 'Religion and Relations between Genders', *Politics and Religion Journal*, Vol. 2, No. 1.

Kim, Sebastian C.H., 2012, 'Conversion', *Hedlund*.

Kooiman, Dick, 1989, *Conversion and Social Equality in India: The London Missionary Society in South Travancore in the 19th Century*, Manohar, Delhi.

Kosambi, Meera (ed.), 2000, *Pandita Ramabai Through Her Own Words: Selected Works*, OUP, Delhi.

Kumar, Ashok and Rowena Robinson, 2010, 'Legally Hindu: Dalit Lutheran Christians of Coastal Andhra Pradesh', in Rowena Robinson and Joseph M. Kuzur (eds), *Margins of Faith: Dalits and Tribal Christianity in India*, Sage, Delhi.

Lalruatkima, 2010, 'TRANS-Formative Possibilities: Tribal Formations in Conversation with Dalit Theology', in Sathianathan Clarke et al. (eds), *Dalit Theology in the Twenty-First Century: Discordant Voices, Discerning Pathways*, OUP, Delhi.

Lobo, Lancy, 2010, 'Christianization, Hinduization and Indigenous Revivalism among the Tribals of Gujarat', in Rowena Robinson and Joseph M. Kuzur (eds), *Margins of Faith: Dalits and Tribal Christianity in India*, Sage, Delhi.

Malhotra, Rajiv, 2011, *Being Different: An Indian Challenge to Western Universalism*, Harper Collins, New Delhi.

Mary, John, 2011, *Indian Catholic Christians and Nationalism: A Study Based on the Official Catholic Journals of the Period 1857–1957*, ISPCK, Delhi.

Mehta, Pratap Bhanu, 2011, 'Hinduism and the Politics of Rights in India', in Thomas Banchoff and Robert Wuthnow (eds), *Religion and the Global Politics of Human Rights*, OUP, Oxford.

Meshak, Samuel W. (ed.), 2007, *Mission with the Marginalized: Life and Witness of Rev. Dr. Prasanna Kumari Samuel*, Christian Sahitya Samiti, Tiruvalla.

Mieth, Dietmar, 2009, 'Meister Eckhart: The Power of Inner Liberation', in Ananta Kumar Giri (ed.), *Modern Prince and the Modern Sage: Transforming Power and Freedom*, Sage, New Delhi, pp. 405–28.

Mosse, David, 2010, 'The Catholic Church and Dalit Christian Activism in Contemporary Tamil Nadu', in Rowena Robinson and Joseph M. Kuzur (eds), *Margins of Faith: Dalits and Tribal Christianity in India*, Sage, Delhi.

Mukherjee, Arun Kumar, 1992, *Keshub Chunder Sen*, Publications Division, Delhi.

Nadkarni, M.V., 2003 [2008], 'Ethics and Relevance of Conversions: A Critical Assessment of Religious and Social Dimensions in a Gandhian Perspective', *Economic and Political Weekly*, Vol. 38, No. 3, pp. 227–35.

——, 2006, *Hinduism: A Gandhian Perspective*, 2nd Edition, Ane Books, New Delhi.

Omvedt, Gail, 2008, *Seeking Begumpura: The Social Vision of Anti-Caste Intellectuals*, Rowman & Littlefield, Delhi.

Painadath, S., 2007, *We are Co-Pilgrims: Towards a Culture of Inter-Religious Harmony*, ISPCK, Delhi.

Pandian, M.S.S., 2010, 'Nation as Nostalgia: The Ambiguous Spiritual Journey of Vengal Chakkarai', in M.T. Ansari and Deeptha Achar (eds), *Discourse, Democracy and Difference: Perspectives on Community, Politics and Culture*, Sahitya Akademi, Delhi.

Patrick, G., 2003, *Religion and Subaltern Agency*, Department of Christian Studies, Chennai.

Prathathu, Paul, 1997, *Ashram Spirituality: A Search Into the Christian Ashram Movement against its Hindu Background*, Satprakashan, Indore.

Rahner, Karl, 1973, 'The Spirituality of the Church of the Future', *Theological Investigations*, Vol. XX.

Rajan, Jesu, 1989, *Bede Griffiths and Sannyasa*, Asia Trading Corporation, Bangalore.

Robinson, Rowena, 2003, *Christians of India*, Sage, Delhi.

Robinson, Rowena and Joseph M. Kuzur (eds) 2010, *Margins of Faith: Dalits and Tribal Christianity in India*, Sage, Delhi.

Rolland, Romain, 1954 [1929], *The Life of Ramakrishna*, Advaita Ashram, Mayavati, Almora.

——, 2012 [1931], *The Life of Vivekananda*, Advaita Ashram, Mayavati, Almora.

Samartha, S.J., 1973, *The Hindu Response to the Unbound Christ*, Christian Literature Society, Chennai.

Schmalz, Mathew N., 2010, 'Broken Mirror: John Masih's Journey from Isaih to Dalit', in Rowena Robinson and Joseph M. Kuzur (eds), *Margins of Faith: Dalits and Tribal Christianity in India*, Sage, Delhi.

Schouten, Jan Peter, 2012, *Jesus as Guru: The Image of Christ among Hindus and Christians in India*, Overseas Press India, Delhi.

Shourie, Arun, 1994, *Missionaries in India: Continuities, Changes, Dilemmas*, ASA Publications, Delhi.

Skolimowski, Henryk, 1991, *Dancing Shiva in the Ecological Age: Heralding the Dawn of Ecological Reconstruction in 21st Century*, Clarion Books, New Delhi.

Thomas, M.M., 1970, *The Acknowledged Christ of the Indian Renaissance*, Christian Literature Society, Madras.

Vattimo, G., 1999, *Belief*, Polity Press, Cambridge.

Wilfred, Felix, 2000, *Asian Dreams and Christian Hopes*, ISPCK, Delhi.

——, 2007, *Dalit Empowerment*, NBCLC, Bangalore.

——, 2009, *Margins: Sites of Asian Theology*, ISPCK, Delhi.

——, 2010, *Asian Public Theology: Critical Currents in Challenging Times*, ISPCK, Delhi.

——, 2012, 'Rice Christians: A Quest for Life', *Hedlund*.

Visvanathan, Susan, 1993, *Missionary Styles and the Problem of Dialogue*, Indian Institute of Advanced Study, Shimla.

——, 2007, *Friendship, Interiority and Mysticism: Essays in Dialogue*, Orient Longman, Hyderabad.

Vivekananda Kendra Prakashan Trust, 2009, *The Wandering Monk*, 2nd Edition, Chennai.

Vivekananda, Swami, 2011 [1900], *Christ the Messenger*, Advaita Ashram, Mayavati, Almora.

Yogananda, Sri Sri Paramahansa, 2007, *The Second Coming of Christ Within You: The Resurrection of Christ within You*, Yugoda Satsanga Society of India, Calcutta.

3

Community Within Community

Politics of Exclusion in the Construction of Sikh Identity

Paramjit S. Judge

The central argument of this article is to emphasize the discrepancy between the claimed and the actual practices of the communities, which theoretically speaking, emerge from the fundamental distinction between religion and community. It has been argued that the hegemonic structure within the community is the major source of both the social hierarchy and the discourse of equality the objective of which is built into the logic of power which expands from informal to the formal levels. For the purpose the case of the Churhas/Mazhabis, who are lowest in the hierarchy of castes in India, has been elaborated to show how the politics of religion is embedded into the hierarchical order of castes within the Sikh community. The discussion been divided into five parts. The first part succinctly outlines essential features of the Sikh community, whereas the second deals with the issue of caste among the Sikhs. The third part takes cognisance of the Mazhabis, whereas the findings of the empirical study of the Mazhabis have been briefly described and examined in the fourth part. The discussion is concluded in the fifth part.

Sikh Community

The Sikhs are the fourth largest religious community in India and have the population of about twenty million persons.[1] Of all the religious communities including the Zoroastrians the Sikhs are the youngest religious community, as Sikhism established itself as a religion in the 18th century though the first Guru of the Sikhs, Guru Nanak Dev, founded the Sikh faith sometimes in the early 16th century. Despite their small size, the Sikhs constitute the majority population in the Indian province of Punjab (60%). The Sikhs, however, are spread all over India and in the world and are among the most prosperous communities in the country. It is evident from the fact that among various religious communities living in rural areas the Sikhs have the second highest mean monthly per capita income at ₹ 864.72 (the Jains have ₹ 978.36) and in the urban areas the Sikhs have the highest expenditure patterns at ₹ 1,498.81 (Thorat 2011). It is clear from the data that the Sikhs have done well in improving their economic conditions after India achieved independence in 1947. There are two factors that have contributed significantly towards their economic prosperity. One, the green revolution – a phenomenon of high agricultural productivity – occurred in Punjab in the second half of the 1960s. Since a majority of the Sikh live in rural areas among whom most of them are peasants, they benefitted from the agrarian change. Secondly, the religious factor of community solidarity has significantly helped them to survive odds and through their hard work they have done well.

There are two salient features of the Sikh community, which are strongly linked to the politics of religion. Firstly, the religious identity of the Sikhs is defined by the state and secondly, there has been a powerful separatist movement among the Sikhs to achieve sovereign state of Khalistan during the last two decades of the previous century. It is interesting to note that the Sikh identity is legally defined (Judge and Kaur 2010) and it happened in 1925 when the British Indian government enacted the Gurdwara Reform Act. The history of the development of Sikhism shows a great degree of diversity in its religious tradition (Oberoi 1993). The role of British policy towards Sikhs has played decisive role in the making of the Sikh identity. As early as the 1880s, Bingley (1985) wrote a book for the purpose of understanding the Sikhs to ascertain how useful they would be as soldiers in the British army. He emphasized the need for saving Sikhism from the powerful influence of Hinduism. The Singh Sabha movement in 1880s emerged in reaction to various challenges emanating from the activities of Christian missionaries as well as the religious enumeration through the census operations by the British Indian government. Singh (2004) argues that the Sikh symbols of identity emerged as a result of negotiation between the British and the Singh Sabha leaders.[2] These symbols were: *Kesh* (unshorn hair), *kanga* (comb), *karha* (iron bangles), *kachha* (breeches), and *kirpan* (sword). Fox (1987) has analysed the way the British constructed the martial races in India and one of them was Sikhs. It is interesting to note that the British strictly imposed the five symbols of Sikh identity in the Sikh regiments exclusively comprised by Sikh soldiers.

The distinct identity of the Sikhs was established in the Act of 1925 which also established a managing body called the Shiromani Gurdwaras Parbandhak Committee (henceforth SGPC) to look after the Sikh historical shrines. The control over the shrines gave unlimited access to the financial resources to the SGPC and consequently, it began to create a homogenous Sikh community called Khalsa by insisting on the five symbols as mandatory for every Sikh.[3] The SGPC has been an elected body of the Sikhs, but to be eligible to vote one has to sign an undertaking that one observes the Sikh principles as prescribed by the SGPC. Over a period of time, the issue of elections has created litigations with regard to whether all Sikhs should have the right to vote in the elections of the religious body or only the Khalsa Sikh should have the privilege (Judge and Kaur 2010). It is interesting to note that the definition of the Sikh in the Act of 1925 applicable to all historical Sikh shrines in Punjab has not been the universally applicable definition of the Sikh. It is clear from the fact that the Delhi Sikh Gurdwaras Act of 1971 does not recognize the person with shorn hair as the Sikh.

It is clear from the discussion on the issue of Sikh identity that the politics is essentially predicated upon the notion of religious community by articulating the constitutive rules as immutable and must be adhered to by all members of the community. At the same time, the practice of politics is located in the production of differences and accepting the two in general. A person becomes Sikh by adhering to the basic principles of Sikh symbols and thus becoming eligible to vote in elections of the religious body, but his/her ineligibility does not imply his/her excommunication form the faith. Even when the constitutive rules of Sikhism are observed, the politics of exclusion embraces the internal caste-based heterogeneity of the community. The issue of caste in the Sikh religion which claims to be egalitarian is not only a social issue but also a political issue.

Mapping Castes among the Sikhs

The caste question in the Sikh community has been both muted and loud – an apparent paradox prevalent as a result of the disjunction between claim and empirical reality. One may argue that such paradoxes could be found among all religions and religious communities. Egalitarian values in Christianity are neutralized by racism in the USA. There is a widespread belief – and that belief has been consistently and continuously claimed to be true – is that Sikhism does not preach caste inequality. Kahn Singh Nabha (1973) and Bhai Vir Singh (Bal 2006) in the 19th century and the SGPC after independence have claimed that there is no caste among the Sikhs. The empirical reality is that among the non-Hindu religious communities, Sikhs are covered under the constitutional provision according to which certain castes among them are identified as Schedule Castes. All such castes are covered under the reservation policy. So far, despite the anti-caste rhetoric, neither the SGPC nor any Sikh leaders have demanded the end of reservation policy for the scheduled caste Sikhs. The existence of castes among the Sikhs has never been an issue of contestation among the intellectuals and academia, for everybody in Punjab – where 75 per cent of the Sikhs live – takes it for granted that Sikhs are divided along caste lines. Various studies on castes among the Sikhs (Singh 1985, Judge 2002 and Puri 2004) have shown that caste system exists among the Sikhs. As a matter of fact any review of literature on caste consists of a section on caste among the non-Hindus. In a way, caste system is now regarded as the feature of Indian sub-continent. However, are caste hierarchies common among all religious communities? It seems that while determining the correspondence and separation among caste hierarchies, it is important to situate Brahmin and the practice of caste endogamy. The Sikh community in Punjab does not have a visible presence of Brahmins, whereas caste endogamy persists and maintained with the threat or use of violence in cases of hypogamous and sometimes hypergamous marriages where the couples have taken an independent decision. The absence of Brahmin in the non-Hindu religious communities structured the caste hierarchy in distinct forms which were different from the Hindu caste hierarchy. How do we understand this difference?

To understand the issue of distinct caste hierarchies, it is important to make a distinction between the ideal construction of caste hierarchy and the empirical reality. The concept of dominant caste, coined by Srinivas (1987), sought to understand deviations from the ideal hierarchical positions of various castes which are fixed under the Varna scheme. Srinivas (1966) maintained that Varna was unchangeable, whereas castes were dynamic. However, despite the concept of Sanskritization according to which a lower caste could improve its status by changing its ways life through emulation, Srinivas looked at these changes merely within the Varna scheme. He separated the notion of dominance from social hierarchy by arguing that certain lower castes could dominate in a region. It implies that even if a caste was able to improve its condition, it continued to occupy the original Varna position, for Varna was fixed and unchangeable. Such a position is theoretically untenable, because it put a permanent moratorium on the claims of Kshatriya Varna among various middle castes. As a matter of fact, the process of Sanskritization did not implicate caste as much as Varna – the evidence of which could be found in a large number of cases where a particular low caste claimed Kshatriya status.

In the case of non-Hindu religious communities, such as Sikhs, the ideological basis of caste was eliminated, but the caste system continued. At the same time the caste hierarchy among the Sikhs could not be understood in the light of Varna scheme, because Sikhism did not share the justification of caste system with Hinduism. As a result of lack of justificatory principles of caste system and the emphasis of the first Sikh Guru on physical labour, a distinct caste hierarchy emerged among the Sikhs in which the owner cultivator and the numerically preponderant caste took the place of upper caste. The Jat Sikhs – Shudra caste in the light of the Hindu tradition – became the upper caste. However, Jats were not the only one who improved their caste status. Other castes such as Tarkhans, Kalals, etc. were also able to remove the low caste stigma and emerged as the major caste groups within the religious community. Such a change could not take place among the low untouchable castes, particularly the Mazhabis.

Mazhabis and Their Exclusion

Among the various low castes, which were later on included in the schedule of the list of depressed castes of the Indian Constitution, were Mazhabis, Ramdasia, Sansis, Bazigars, Julahas, Meghs, etc. However, most of these castes were also comprised by members who did not convert to Sikhism. Interestingly, some of these castes converted to different religions among which the Churha/Bhangis were the most prominent. The Hindu Churha became Balmiki, Sikh was called Mazhabis, the Muslim was known as Mussali, and the Christian was christened as Masih. However, the Mazhabis and the Balmikis were more prominent than others. Masihs are now designated as the backward class, whereas the Hindu and Sikh Churhas are included among the Scheduled Castes. According to the Census of India, 2001, the total population of Mazhabis Sikhs is 22, 20,945, whereas the number of Balmikis is 7,85,464. Since most of the Muslim Churha might have remained in or migrated to

Pakistan in 1947, there is no way of estimating it. On the other hand, their conversion to Christianity has been so overwhelming in contrast to other caste communities that Christians and Churha have become coterminous in the popular expressions among the upper caste people. If we assume that all the Christians of Punjab belong to the Churha caste, which is not the case, then we can say that there are 2,92,800 persons of Churha caste who are Christians. Thus we can have the following figures presented in Table 1.

Table 1

Population of Churhas according to religion and religious nomenclature

Category	*Total Population*	*Percentage*
Mazhabis (Sikh)	22,20,945	67.32
Balmikis (Hindus)	7,85,464	23.81
Masih (Christians)	2,92,800	8.87
Total	32,99,209	100

Source: Census of India, 2001.

Earlier information regarding the population of Mazhabis' Sikhs is available in the census records. Webster (2007) has worked out the data covering 50 years starting from 1881 till 1931. According to the figures provided by him, the total population of the Mazhabis/Sikh Churhas was 1,69,247 in 1931.

Among the Scheduled Caste Sikhs the Mazhabis are an overwhelming majority, but more interesting is the fact that more than two-third of the total members of the Churha caste are Sikhs. The Mazhabis are also concentrated in the major pockets of Punjab, particularly Amritsar, Bathinda, Mansa, Firozpur, etc. On the other hand, the Balmikis are concentrated in the Doaba region. Interestingly, whereas the Balmikis are concentrated in the urban areas of Punjab, the Mazhabis live in villages. By occupation the Mazhabis are involved in agriculture and were siris under the traditional sepidari system in villages.[4] Their women had been working in the houses of the landowners as sweepers. The Balmikis living in the rural

Punjab were almost similar to their Sikh counterparts. However, in urban areas they were mostly sweepers. In a recently conducted study it was found that the Balmikis as well as the Mazhabis have diversified their economic activities, though a major section among them is involved in the occupations which they had been doing for a long time (Judge and Bal 2009). If we specifically focus on women (both Mazhabi and Balmiki), changes are far more limited than men. In villages Mazhabi women are largely doing the job of sweepers in the houses of upper caste landowners. In certain cases they have become domestic help as cooks, which, from the point of view of commensality, is a major change.

The Balmiki/Mazhabi women have started undertaking certain measures to restructure their symbolic universe. Most of those who are working as domestic servants have stopped cleaning the toilets. Interestingly, unlike the earlier vocation of carrying the night soil on their heads, which was demeaning and humiliating work, cleaning modern toilets does not carry such a stigma. Avoiding or refusing such work is a negation and rejection of the humiliating work which symbolizes centuries' old subjugation and dehumanization.

We may now turn our attention to a significant anthropological aspect which has tremendous heuristic value. It seems that the lower castes never accepted their low caste position and the evidence is found in their symbolic universe. It may be underlined that the low castes have large number of stories in the form of myths and legends which depict the mode of their fall in the caste hierarchy. Obviously, all the narratives also inform that the concerned caste was earlier occupying the higher caste status. Two of such narratives may be stated here before taking up the same issue in the case of Churhas. Deliége has collected myths of origin of various low castes in Tamil Nadu. Let us narrate two of these myths thus

> Two brothers went to a temple to conduct a prayer ceremony (*jabbam*). On their way, they found the remains of dead cow. As the younger brother was weak and small, the elder proposed to remove carcass himself. The people present told

> him that he should conduct the prayer session instead, but he answered: *Een thambi pappaan*. The people understood that his younger brother was a Brahmin, *paappaan*. To thank the elder brother for his work, God blessed him a Paraiyar, whereas the younger brother became a Brahmin. (1999: 74)

The following myth brings out the story of origin quite clearly:

> Once four Brahmin brothers were going to a fair. On their way, they had to cross a river, but as they came to the river, they saw a cow stuck in the mud by the bank. One by one, they tried to extricate the cow from the mud by the bank. As the younger was pulling on the tail of the cow trying to get it out, the cow died. As the younger brother was touching the cow when it died, his brothers considered him to be unclean and had nothing to do with him from then on. The present-day Camars [sic] are descendants of this outcasted Brahmin. (ibid.: 85)

These two myths, in essence lead us to the notion of fall, which is related to cow either dead or in trouble and dying. In this regard, the creators of this myth have advertently or inadvertently accepted the Brahminic tradition of pollution and purity. Touching the dead cow does not only pollute the person, but also degrades him irreversibly. The second important insight one gets from these myths is that these untouchable castes originated from the higher caste, that is, Brahmin. Thirdly, the fall had occurred without any conscious violation of religious principles. In other words, the degradation of their forefather to the low caste occurred without him being guilty of any violation. The story of upper caste origin and the myth of fall constitute the most significant elements in the construction of anthropological past by these castes.

Similar attempt has also been made by Ashok (2001) in his work with regard to Churhas. According to him, Balmikis, Chandal and Dhanik castes emerged as result of hypogamous marriage between Shudra man and Brahmin woman. Before the arrival of Aryans, Ashok (ibid.: 9) informs that Dravidian were living in Punjab. One of the castes among the Dravidians was known as 'Churhamani', which was a warrior caste. The people of this caste always kept weapons with them owing to which they were called Dhaniks and they were responsible for the protection of the country. The word Dhanik means the one who carries *Dhanush* (bow and arrow). When the Aryans invaded this region, the rich Dravidians left the place and Churhamani were left behind. Owing to their small number, they could not continue to fight against the Aryans. Over a period of time, the Aryan rulers pushed them to the bottom of the society.

The above narration of Ashok is no different from those of myths from the South India in respect of the story of 'fall'. They also claim to be once occupying upper caste status though unlike the low castes of South India, who claimed to be Brahmins, they alleged that they were Kshatriyas. The major difference is the reason for 'fall' – an important difference seems to be connected with the specific upper caste status. The fall of Brahmin is in line with the myth of touching carcass of cow, whereas the myth of degradation of Kshatriya caste people is woven around ostensibly historical occurrences of loss in war and subsequent subjugation of the warrior class. In the contemporary cultural moorings of Punjab the construction of Mazhabis Sikh as brave and aggressive tends to lend tremendous support to such a mythical narrative. It is important to note that irrespective of valorization of tradition by Mazhabis writers, the Mazhabis as brave and aggressive is a widely accepted point of view, opinion or stereotype. The involvement of Mazhabis in feuds between the Jat landowning families is regarded as an indispensable fact. It is important to elaborate this aspect of social anthropology of Punjabi society.

Pettigrew (1978) in her study of Jat Sikhs of Punjab has shown the intertwining of village level factional feuds and state politics. The Jats, who are mostly Sikhs, are landowners of Punjab. They employ the Mazhabis as their attached workers under the sepidari/jajmani system. Under the sepidari system the families of Jat and Mazhabis are connected to each other for many generations. Along with the Mazhabis male head of the household, his wife also works in the house of the landowner. The sepidari system started declining after the green revolution when cash economy replaced the traditional mode of payments in kind. Mechanization of agriculture further weakened the system. However, the major change occurred as a result of the emergence of better opportunities outside agriculture. Despite all these changes, its practice continues to a limited extent (Judge 2009). The distinctiveness of the sepidari system actually operating between the Jat landowners and the Mazhabis workers from its usual practice in Punjab in general has been the involvement of the Mazhabis in the interfamily feuds of the landowners. Since these feuds continued for generations, the Mazhabis remained equally involved. It is a popular saying in Punjab that no murder takes place without the participation of Mazhabis. Such an attachment of the Balmikis in villages of Doaba is absent.

It is also important to mention that there have been a regiment of Mazhabis in the Indian Army known as the Sikh Light Infantry (Sikh Li). The tradition was started by the British as early as 1857 when 12,000 Mazhabis soldiers were raised to lay siege to Delhi (Puri 2004). The caste prevailed even in such recruitments despite the British recognition to the bravery of the Mazhabis. Puri (ibid.: 200–1) writes,

> Mazhabis constituted Mazhabi regiments – the Sikh Pioneers 23, 32, and 34, later named 'Sikh Light Infantry' – separate and distinguished from exclusively Jat Sikh Regiments. No Sikh Jat or any other caste man could be recruited in the Sikh Light Infantry. Conversely, in the Sikh regiments, as an old retired Brigadier explained to the author, 'not even a Labana Sikh be recruited to the Sikh regiments'. The fear of pollution of the high castes could compromise their loyalty. However, association with the army gave a boost to the Mazhabi's sense of dignity, marking them out in distinction to the other untouchable castes.

It may be noted that the valiant Mazhabi image was not solely sustained by their recruitment to the British army. It was the participation of the Mazhabis in the Akali movement in the second and third decades of 20th century that reinforced their image. The following observations of Hares have been cited from Webster (2007: 144):

> During the Akali agitation many thousands of Sikhs had been thrown into prison for their lawless behaviour, and in order to fill the ranks of the Akali Shahidi Jathas or Bands of Martyrs, the Sikh leaders welcomed warmly anyone and everyone who would help their cause in any way. Many thousands of Chuhras, the outcaste farm labourers of the province, joined them and, adopting all outward marks of Sikhism, were enrolled as the *Mazhabi* Sikhs. But when the Akalis had attained their object they had no further use for the *Mazhabis*, and the latter returned to their villages, disappointed and disillusioned, to find themselves still treated as outcastes, forbidden to draw water from the village wells, or to enter the Sikh temples, or to take part in the social life of the Sikhs.

The struggle for better status among the lower castes has taken many routes one of which is religious conversion. The conversion to Sikhism has created a distinct caste of Mazhabis who have distinguished themselves from their Hindu Balmiki counterparts. Has religious conversion brought about changes in the status of the Mazhabis? What is the perception of the Mazhabis with regard to their social status within the Sikh community? Are they experiencing exclusion in social and religious spaces? What is the nature of exclusion of Mazhabis?

Is it a product of social inequality of castes? Is there religious exclusion felt and experienced by the Mazhabis within the Sikh community? What is the form and content of these exclusions of Mazhabis? It was in the context of these queries that data were collected by administering an interview schedule in the villages of Amritsar and Gurdaspur districts. According to the information provided by the Census 2001, the Mazhabis are concentrated in Amritsar, Ferozepur and Bathinda (including Mansa) districts. The area of Gurdaspur district adjoining Amritsar district also has high concentration of the Mazhabis.

A total of 140 Mazhabis' respondents from ten villages, five each in Amritsar and Gurdaspur districts, were randomly selected and interviewed. Five villages in Amritsar district are Janiyai, Nangal, Mahal, Jeewan Singh Nagar, and Preet Nagar. In the case of Gurdaspur district, the villages are Bhumbli, Alawalpur, Babari Nangal, Alowal, and Khunda. The information about these villages which was collected in each village was regarding the number of gurdwaras and caste basis, if any, of these gurdwaras. As we shall just see, gurdwaras were linked with caste. Let us start with the villages of Amritsar. In Janiyai there were three gurdwaras out of which one was owned and run by Jat Sikhs, whereas two gurdwaras were of the Mazhabis. Nangal consisted of two Mazhabis gurdwaras and one Jat gurdwara, whereas in village Mahal there were five gurdwaras of Mazhabis and two Jat gurdwaras. Jeewan Nagar, an exclusive Mazhabis settlement had two gurdwaras, whereas in Preet Nagar there were two Mazhabis gurdwaras and three upper caste gurdwaras. In Bhumbli village of Gurdaspur district two Jat gurdwaras, two Mazhabis gurdwaras and one gurdwara of the Kumhar (potters) caste unambiguously depicted the caste basis of gurdwaras in villages. However, Alawalpur village did not have any Mazhabi gurdwara though there were two Jat gurdwaras and one belonged to other castes. Same was the case of Babari Nangal where two Jat gurdwaras and one other gurdwara meant for other non-Jat Sikhs showed caste divisions in place of worship. Alowal had only one Jat gurdwara, whereas one Jat, one Kumhar and one Mazhabis' gurdwara each was in existences in village Khunda.

The information regarding the existence of gurdwaras in the study villages shows caste-wise division among the villagers, but at the same time, it depicts separate localities of various castes. United by religion, villagers are divided by caste. How do the caste-divided villagers create religious divisions through exclusionary practices? So far as their social profile was concerned, the following picture emerged: The Mazhabis respondents belonged to all age groups ranging between 21 and 80 years with the mean age of 42 years. In terms of education, though majority (75.71%) of them were educated, yet very few of them (3.37%) had got education above school level. It clearly shows that though illiteracy is declining, the Mazhabis are not acquiring education which is critical for the radical change in their occupational status. As discussed earlier, Mazhabis are largely involved in agricultural labour either as daily wage labourers or attached labourers under the sepidari/jajmani system. In the changing socio-economic conditions, due to the penetration of capitalism, the traditional economic formations have more or less declined, but the Mazhabis are still involved in low status occupations. Businessmen, doctors and school teachers constituted only five per cent of the respondents, whereas the rest of them were involved in the low status occupations. It is clear from the socio-economic profile of the Mazhabis that most of them are still low in education and high prestige occupations.

Identity and Exclusion

One of the crucial elements in the profile of the respondents is related to their religious identity – the issue shrouded in controversies with claims and counterclaims. Earlier parts in this article have already underlined the significance of five symbols in the making of the Sikh identity. One of the Sikh traditions emphasizes *bana* (dress) and *bani* (writings of the Gurus) as equally important dimensions of the Sikh identity. It was important to know the appearance of the Mazhabis respondents. Interestingly, 35 per cent of them had unshorn hair implying that majority of the respondents have deviated from the standard prescribed identity of the Sikhs.

As a corollary to the above mentioned logic, it was important that we inquire about respondents' own perception of what makes a person Sikh. They were asked to define who is a Sikh? It is interesting to note that most of the respondents were ambivalent towards the identity of the Sikh. Almost half of them gave answers, such as 'I believe in and follow the tenth Guru', 'Granth Sahib' or 'Gurus and *nitnaim*' (Sikh Religious Routine). These respondents did not give priority to the appearance. However, these responses could be interpreted as definitive in terms of appearance. A Sikh may say following the tenth Guru or Guru Granth Sahib corresponds with the tradition of keeping unshorn hair. Since these responses cannot be unambiguously put into a neat category, it may be held that these responses are inclusive in terms of religious identity. For example, love for humanity is a desirable trait in every person, but cannot be taken, as stated by 3.57 per cent of the respondents, as the basis of Sikh identity. Religious identities are not constituted by the universal principles of justice, equality, truth, etc. Any religious identity is based on exclusive definitive traits largely in terms of beliefs and certain cultural/ritual practices.

The Sikh construction of Khalsa during the 19th century attaches great significance to five symbols. The baptism ceremony alleged to be initiated by the tenth Guru in 1699 got the central space in defining the Sikh traditions. It is thus natural that we know the views of the Mazhabis respondents with regard to the significance of five symbols in the Sikh identity. To situate five symbols at their proper place in Mazhabi consciousness, two important aspects have been examined. The first is to know their opinion regarding these symbols, whereas the other is to inquire whether there is a particular symbol which is central in defining the identity of Sikh. The responses were quite interesting as about 45 per cent of them attributed symbolic importance to five symbols, but these were also considered important for the baptized/amritdhari Sikhs by 17.86 per cent of the respondents. It is thus clear that most of the Mazabi respondents did not think that five symbols were crucial and indispensable for the Sikhs to keep.

The SGPC, originally formed to manage historical gurdwaras after the enactment of the Gurdwara Reform Act, 1925, has now turned into the sole agency with the monopoly to handle ecclesiastical issue of Sikhism. From time to time, the SGPC has been issuing *hukamnamas* (orders) to define various dimensions of the Sikh issues including the questioning of Sikh identity. The Mazhabis respondents were asked to describe the SGPC and its role in the lives of the Sikhs. The rationale behind seeking this query was to not only know the level of their awareness, but also their sense of belongingness to the Sikh institution. An inclusive approach of the SGPC would definitely create a sense of belongingness among the members of community. In a way, just more than half of the respondents correctly understood the role of the SGPC in terms of management of gurdwaras. At the same time, two-fifth of the Mazabi respondents seemed to be either indifferent or hostile to the SGPC. There is a reasonable basis to argue that the role of the SGPC could be put under scanner so far as its democratic and egalitarian practices are concerned.

One of the important dimensions of the democratic ethos of the Sikh body (SGPC) is that there are periodic elections that take place after every five years. Even before 1947 since its inception, different political parties used to participate in the SGPC elections. For example, Sohan Singh Josh, the veteran communist leader, was the elected member of the SGPC. After independence there has been a decline in its democratic spirit through systematic attempts at redefining the meaning of Sikh. As a result, the SGPC has been consistently excluding and depriving people professing Sikhism from the voting rights in its elections. When the respondents were asked whether they had voted in the SGPC elections, 65 per cent of them told that had never voted despite the fact that they claimed to be Sikhs. Situating the definition of Sikh provided by the SGPC in the broader Sikh context requires an examination of how the Sikhs define themselves and their religious identity. It is worthwhile to examine the definition and multiple shades of Sikhs as these empirically exist.

There is a gap between the ideal and reality and it is a result of how the world is seen empirically and how it actually exists. The division of the world into sacred and profane may not necessarily demarcate boundaries between socially constructed routine life and religious living. Religion has strong propensity to transverse lines of demarcation between the two. Religion acquires this tendency as it is based on the notion of an infallible world that could only emanate from god and its moral vision. People are not perfect and their world is equally imperfect. Need to govern and control their actions, for the survival is the most essential value in the life. From it emerge various kinds of imperfections and movement away from the strict moral code provided by religion. Thus emerge differences of opinion regarding religious identity though central element in the definition of Sikh is keeping unshorn hair. We find that the dominant view is liberal and provides for lot of variations. The respondent who took a very narrow and definite view of the Sikh identity were only 12.14 per cent.

It is equally important to examine how the Mazhabis understand and respond to those persons who claim to be Sikhs but trim/shave their hair. Interestingly, there are more than one-fourth of the respondents who stated quite categorically that without unshorn hair a person could not be Sikh, whereas 45.71 per cent of the respondents were clear that such persons could claim to be Sikhs but they could not be the Singhs of the Guru. However, despite a degree of Catholicism and liberal attitude with regard to the definition of Sikh, the issue of unshorn hair occupies a central place in the discourse of Sikh identity. In other words, there is a degree of ambivalence towards the Sikh identity, which is handled by emphasizing the crucial importance of the Gurus and their writings (bani) which are personified in the Guru Granth Sahib – the sacred book of the Sikhs.

The presence of castes among the Sikhs is an issue which sometimes create strong reaction among the Sikh establishment only in such situations where attempts are made to make Sikhism coterminous with Hinduism. The fact that there is a provision of reservation for the Scheduled Caste Sikhs, it implies that the Sikh leadership accepts the existence of castes in the Sikh community in principle. The Mazhabis are the Scheduled Caste and they are eligible for the preferential treatment under the reservation policy. What are the experiences and perceptions of the respondents with regard to caste is an important issue for examination. What emerges from the data is highly expected. An overwhelming majority of the respondents (80%) was clear about the castes. Obviously the discourse of equality within the community has struck some roots. However, asking a question whether caste exists among the Sikhs is not a very right kind of query, because there is no need to ask this question. The Indian state through its Constitution acknowledges castes among Sikhs.

One of the arguments is that there is existence of caste-based discrimination against the Mazhabis at religious places. Judge and Bal (2009) noted that the Mazhabis were not permitted to carry the sacred book, Guru Granth Sahib, to their homes arguing that they were dirty and they could violate the *maryada* (code of conduct) of properly keeping the book. However, this was not the only reason. It was also found by them that each separate gurdwara is located in one locality. Since the Mazhabis have their own separate locality, they also had their own gurdwara. In other words, the Mazhabis have constructed their own gurdwaras due to various reasons and caste based discrimination is one of the major reasons. When the Mazhabis respondents were asked about why they had their own separate gurdwara, they give different reasons. Two main reasons for the separate gurdwaras of the Mazhabis could be understood along the lines discussed above. The most important is the discrimination against the Mazhabis in the upper caste gurdwaras followed by the rationale of locality. Almost half of the respondents did not give any clear reason, but avoided indulging into the issue of caste-based religious discrimination.

In conclusion, it may be stated that despite the historical intimacy of the Mazhabis with the Sikh tradition, particularly the tenth Guru, they are at the margin of the religious community. One Mazhabis leader also became the president of the SGPC, but their inclusion in the Sikh community as equals is far from realization. They feel excluded with regard to the SGPC elections and representation.

Concluding Discussion

The detailed discussion of what has been described and examined is required to bring out the issue of the politics of religious exclusion in its rightful historical and social context. Two important issues emerge from the earlier discussion and require further elaboration. These issues become important and essential to be tackled in the light of the fact that the Sikhism is egalitarian in theory and its leaders continue to claim to be so despite obvious empirical evidence. Keeping in view the fundamental distinction between religion and community, what makes the issue worthy of analysis is that the discrimination and exclusion are maintained within the framework caste in one of the cases, whereas the other implicates the political economy of religion. First, the Sikh identity was constructed by the state through enactment and the Sikh is defined by law and not by faith. As part of the state intervention the SGPC was created which began to manage not only the Sikh shrines but also the identity issue. The result was that two discourses were created in identifying the Sikh. One was related with the right to vote in the SGPC elections and the second was the exercise of vote in the political elections at the province and country levels. Both the SGPC and the Legislative Assembly in Punjab are under the control of one political party, that is, the Shiromani Akali Dal (henceforth SAD). At the time of provincial elections the Sikh is defined by the SAD on the basis of faith in the sacred book, whereas in the case of the SGPC elections the voting rights are limited to a much smaller number of Sikhs. The politics of exclusion is practiced in maintaining and sustaining the differences in identity making it a contentious issue within the community.

The second issue is the prevalence of the caste system and the exclusion of certain castes from equal participation in all walks of life thus denying them the opportunities of a good quality life. In order to make sense of the exclusion of Mazhabis, we need to examine the symbolic universe of caste system in general and its implications for the Sikh community believed to be based on the discourse of equality. Dumont (1998) constructed the binary model of pure and impure castes based on the principle of pollution. Accordingly, the castes which pollute and which are polluted are located in a system of hierarchy based on the Hindu texts. However, what is the basis of purity and impurity did not get needed attention from Dumont. It is my contention that the binary opposition between the physical and non-physical labour has been the principle located in hierarchy constructed on the two broad divisions of pure and impure (Judge 2002).[5] Despite the occupational diversity within the caste, underlined in many studies, physical labour remained the basic principle of separation of various castes. For example, a Brahmin or a Rajput could be landowner, but he never tilled the land. Sikhism which emerged as a result of interaction between Hinduism and Islam in late medieval period was based on the fundamental principle of equality. It paved the way for the rise in the status of certain lower castes, particularly the cultivating castes located in the Shudra Varna the most notable among them were the Jats. However, the rise of peasant castes in the caste hierarchy in the Sikh community simultaneously accompanied by the emergence of new hierarchy in which the erstwhile low castes of the peasants occupied the dominant position without changing the status of the castes located at the lowest rungs of the Sikh community. The Mazhabis, who were located at the lowest rung of the Sikh community continued to face discrimination though they changed their occupation from scavenging to agricultural labour/landless cultivators.

Whereas the hegemonic structure perpetuates the dominance of the upper caste Jats, the practice of democracy provides the semblance of equality and consensus within the Sikh community. The perpetuation of difference is marked by the politics of exclusion within the Sikh community. Difference is political when it is irreversibly connected with power and status. Even when the claim of achieving inclusive community is made, it is expected that it is based on achievement of equality with difference. The politics of difference in the case of the Sikh community is upheld by the articulation of the discourse of equality which is stated to have originated from the founders of the faith making it irrefutable and beyond doubt. Therefore, exclusion and difference become inseparable in the internal institutional and social practices of the Sikh community.

Notes

1. Hindus, Muslims and Christians are followed by the Sikhs in population.

2. The Singh Sabha movement carried out the propagation of the Sikh faith and made an attempt to create a homogenous community by removing various parallel traditions from the mainstream.
3. The Jajmani/Sepidari system is a system of economic interdependence among castes wherein the lower service castes provide services to the landowners and in turn are paid in kind at the harvesting season.
4. In certain ways, it could be equated to the institution of inquisition initiated by the Roman Catholic Church in medieval Europe. However, the SGPC does not have the power to physically punish the people. The methods used are to deny the unorthodox Sikh the access to certain resources and privileges.
5. However, swordsmanship and cooking could be exceptions making physical labour as impure.

References

Arifi, Naranajan, 1999, *Ranghretian Da Itihas*, Literature House, Amritsar.

Ashok, Samsher Singh, 2001, *Mazabi Sikhan da Itihas*, Bhai Chattar Singh Jiwan Singh, Amritsar.

Bal, Gurpreet, 2006, 'Construction of Gender and Religious Identities in the First Punjabi Novel *Sundari*', *Economic and Political Weekly*, Vol. 41, No. 32, 12–18 August, pp. 3528–34.

Bingley, A.H., 1985, *The Sikhs*, National Book Shop, Delhi.

Deliége, Robert, 1999, *The Untouchables of India*, Berg, New York.

Dumont, Louis, 1998, *Homo Hierarchicus: The Caste System and Its Implications*, OUP, Delhi.

Fox, Richard G., 1987, *Lions of Punjab: Culture in the Making*, Archives Publishers, New Delhi.

Jevtic, Miroljub, 2007, 'Political Science and Religion', *Politics and Religion Journal*, Vol. 1, No. 1.

——, 2008, 'Religion and Relations between Genders', *Politics and Religion Journal*, Vol. 2, No. 1.

Judge, Paramjit S., 2002, 'Religion, Caste and Communalism in Punjab', *Sociological Bulletin*, Vol. 51, No. 2.

——, 2009, *Social Exclusion in Rural Punjab*, Research Report, Centre for the Study of Social Exclusion and Inclusive Policy, Guru Nanak Dev University, Amritsar.

Judge, Paramjit S. and Gurpreet Bal, 2009, *Mapping Dalits: Contemporary Reality and Future Prospects*, Rawat Publications, Jaipur.

Judge, Paramjit S. and Manjit Kaur, 2010, 'Politics of Sikh Identity: Understanding Religious Exclusion', *Sociological Bulletin*, Vol. 59, No. 3, pp. 345–66.

Nabha, Kahn Singh, 1973, *Hum Hindu Nahin*, Singh Sabha Shatabdi Committee, Amritsar (First Published in 1898).

Oberoi, Harjot, 1993, *The Construction of Religious Boundaries: Culture, Identity and Diversity in the Sikh Tradition*, OUP, New Delhi.

Pettigrew, Joyce, 1978, *Robber Noblemen: A Study of the Political System of the Sikh Jats*, Ambika Publications, New Delhi.

Puri, Harish K., 2004, 'The Scheduled Castes in the Sikh Community: A Historical Perspective', in Harish K. Puri (ed.), *Dalits in Regional Context*, Rawat Publications, Jaipur.

Ram, Pandit Bakhshi, nd, *Mera Jeevan Sangharash* (My Life Struggle), Punjab Pradesh Balmik Sabha, Jalandhar.

Singh, Jagjit, 1985, *Perspectives on Sikh Studies*, Guru Nanak Foundation, New Delhi.

Singh, Pashaura, 2004, 'Sikh Identity in the Light of History: A Dynamic Perspective', in Pashaura Singh and N. Gerald Barrier (eds.), *Sikhism and History*, OUP, New Delhi.

Srinivas, M.N., 1966, *Social Change in Modern India*, Allied Publishers, Bombay.

——, 1987, *The Dominant Caste and Other Essays*, OUP, New Delhi.

Thorat, Amit, 2011, 'Religions and Development, India', Working Paper Series, Vol. 2, No. 1, Indian Institute of Dalit Studies, Delhi.

4

Religious Landscape, Low Caste Hindus and the Identity Politics

Configuration of Socio-religious Space for Weaker Sections in Jammu City, J&K (India)

Ashish Saxena and Vijaylaxmi Saxena

It is seen that the dawning of a new century has not been accompanied by the eclipse of religiosity among individuals and in public culture rather because of disenchantment with our increasingly rationalized society, religion continues to provide meaning and intertwine daily social, economic and political activity of human world. The societal rites of the past are replaced by the religious practices in modern world and thus there occurs a simultaneous increase in the number of rites across the calendar, i.e. a shift in the contours of social time. The proliferation of rites and dispersion of the sacred thus encourage a more disciplined and even distribution of emotional energies over a wider spectrum of activities (Fenn 2001: 120–25). Similarly, Jürgen Habermas has given considerable attention over his long career to the question of religion in modern society. Habermas replaced the hope for 'disappearance' with a call for 'privatization'. In texts such as *Post-Metaphysical Thinking* (1988) he reminded his readers that religion is an existential necessity that is 'indispensable in ordinary life'. In the face of suffering, it is only natural for people to turn to faith. Later, Habermas supported the notion of 'publicization', stressed that religion should not be limited to the private sphere. Rather, it should intervene in the public sphere and use its founding documents and traditions to refine 'moral intuitions'. This third phase of Habermas' thought predicts the coming of a 'post-secular society', in which individuals, without abdicating their autonomy, rediscover a sense of transcendence and religious belonging (see Portier 2011). Thus, religion reflected the nature of the social system within which it is expressed. The universality of religion suggests that it corresponds to some deep and probably inescapable human need. Thus, rather than disappearing in an age of reason, religion seemed destined to transform itself. In the modern period, religion is no longer confined to an institutional form and took on a plurality of expressions including radical environmentalism, eco-feminism, holistic therapies and human potential groups, as communism, socialism and nationalism had taken on in the past.

Alongside, the popular religiosity is an important contemporary trend encompassing the world religions: Buddhism, Christianity, Hinduism, Islam, and Judaism. This is not to claim that popular religion is replacing mainstream religion; rather, for some people, popular religious forms offer viable alternatives. Fundamentalist and cultural groups are vehicles of popular religion. The former engage in the process of negotiating cultural transition, where the identity of certain groups is, according to group members, menaced during major cultural transitions; the latter, in contrast, function as organizations of cultural defence against challenges from unwelcome, intrusive, alien forces. In both cases, religion provides resources for negotiating transitions or asserting a new claim to a sense of worth; both involve political responses. Popular religions are community expressions of group desire to achieve a religious, social and political satisfaction not forthcoming from mainstream religions. In sum, popular religious organizations offer ways of affirming the autonomy and identity of a religious or ethno-religious community, especially in urban centres where traditional community ties are often sundered. Popular religion reflects the power of ordinary people to take charge of their own spiritual, and in some cases, material well-being. Because it is the religion of the 'ordinary' people, it is usually quite different in both conception and form to the religious orthodoxies propounded by the leaders of hegemonial religions (Haynes 1997). Modernity, technology and religion one of the widest refrains in the social sciences in the latter half of the 20th century must have been the secularization thesis that modernity has led to the substitution of religious traditions with rationalism, scientism and individualism. Public life, it is argued, has been secularized and that which is religious has been privatized (Kurtz 1995).

In south Asian countries like India, the impact of modernization too has led to the emergence of new religions, revivals, and reforms within the great traditions. In modern societies, with their complex fabric of social differentiations, not only among religion, but other groups and social activities, there appears a proliferation of rites. Since many rites are attached to the practices of specific groups and do not take on a societal-wide role, this proliferation does not necessarily impede societal integration. Even those rites that are societalized are combined with others in a larger number, with a reduced emotionality for each. The sum of societal rites themselves become routinized and more fully integrated into the workaday fabric of social order, reaching a variety of accommodations with other institutional spheres such as the state, the workplace, the market, the ethnic group, and the family (Fenn 2001: 120–25).

Keeping in view the above discussions, the present work aims at exploring the spatial expansion of subaltern groups in urban setting; socio-religious mobility among lower caste Hindus and the creation of sacred and secular space vis-à-vis higher Hindu caste groups in a sacred traditional Indian city, i.e. Jammu city in Jammu and Kashmir state. The paper, in brief, explores the changing landscape of lower castes areas of worship and settlement, histories of their mobility, identity assertion and changing relationships.

Intersection of Space, Religion and Politics

The study of religion as a force in people's adaptation to and creation of landscape is certainly a proper and important endeavour in the field of sociology of religion. Landscape, in a very broad sense, conveys the idea of land utilization and development by people, and it is important to realize that ideologies, for example, religious beliefs, are crucial in the direction and accomplishment of this process. In turn, landscape formation affects the development of such beliefs.

Human use of the environment has not only been directed towards people, it has also been oriented towards the sacred (Levine 1986). Religion, that is, experience of the supernatural, is an important motivating force in peoples' lives. Isaac suggests that there have been four groups of geographical studies which have dealt with religion (Isaac 1963). One group deals with the effect of religion on cultural landscapes or regions; another studies religious structures, their locations, sites and orientations and designs; another considers demographic issues such as the distribution of religious groups, and the last group attempts theoretical arguments which seek to define the concerns of the geography of religion of which the work of Deffontaines (1953) and Sopher (1967) would be examples.

Whereas Sopher's (1967) consideration of the spatial expression of religious phenomena could lead to a descriptive mode of apprehending the religious quest, his appreciation of the ecology of religion heralds a potentially dialectical method of analysis which would see religion as social force and social expression. In brief, religion is a deeply personalized yet inter-subjective inspection of ultimately intimate and important questions and it is an institutionalized force which both legitimates and challenges social relations in society.

Increasingly, geographers have explored the politics of religious space, drawing attention particularly to the tensions between sacred and secular use and among religious groups over (often) urban space (Kong 2001). Within geographies of religion, it has been acknowledged that sacred space is contested space, just as the sacred is a 'contested category' (Needham, cit. in Chidester and Linenthal 1995). Characteristic of sacred space are 'hierarchical power relations of domination and subordination, inclusion and exclusion, appropriation and dispossession', involving 'entrepreneurial, social, political and other profane forces' (ibid.: 17). Altogether, they constitute a politics of sacred space, in which power relations define sacredness of space.

Religion, Caste and Identity politics in India

Communities are often characterized by various forms of oppression, 'protecting the prevailing value system including its moral code' (Smith 1999). There is also an 'intolerance of difference', since the 'ideal of community' relies on a desire for 'the same social wholeness and identification' (Young 1990 a and b). This is precisely the differentiation within modernity.

Locating the political connotation of 'identity' vis-à-vis religion it is interesting to find that even the identity theory links contemporary religion to identity in order to provide a comprehensive frame of reference for the large amount of data about religion in the social sciences discourse. The renewed interest in identity and the construction of knowledge from the 1990s onwards has provoked a shift from considering communities as 'given' to investigating the power relations and discourses by which they are constantly defined and redefined (Pernau 2005). Adding further complexity to the community identity issue is the power play of religion in the contemporary world.

In the developing nations like India, the multiplicity of groups and tradition and various characters of their inter-relations provide much of the richness to Indian culture. The varieties of social collectivities such as castes, religion, class, clan, communities, and interest groups have tended to be shaped in the name of ethnic and social identities. With the above backdrop, religion vis-à-vis identity politics appears to be a sensitive issue both at global and regional level. Thus it is high time to study the status of religio-cultural practices in the modern world and to identify their relevance in contemporary society. Referring Kothari's (1970: 232) statement that – 'we shall examine the relationships between caste and politics as basically a relationship for the specific purpose of organizing public activity'; we also see the relationship between community and religion in the similar fashion.

Simultaneously, on the question of caste Kothari (1970: 229) rightly points that, everyone recognizes that the social system in India is organized around caste structures and caste identities. In dealing with the relationship between caste and politics, however, the tendency is to start at the wrong end of the question: Is caste disappearing? In reality, however, no social system disappears. A more useful point of departure would be: What form is caste taking under the impact of politics, and what form is politics taking in a caste-oriented society? A few who are free from a dichotomous view of caste and politics and are prepared to look into precise empirical relations suffers from another preconception and often a contrary theoretical construct. ... Politics, in this view, is an instrument wielded by a particular stratum in society to consolidate or raise its position; its function is to reproduce, or modify, existing states of superior-subordinate relationships. Such an approach blurs understanding of the developmental reality which consists not in any approximation to a preconceived framework but in the changing interactions of the constituent elements in a dynamic situation. But in the particular case of caste and politics, even this is only partly relevant. Where caste itself becomes a political category, it is futile to argue as to whether caste uses politics or politics uses caste (ibid.: 230).

It may not be wrong to say that religion has been, and continues to be, a matter of absorbing interest for many in India still today. In former centuries no aspect of life was set apart from religion. All social relations were inevitably and legitimately suffused with religious ideas and acts. The possibility of religion in a modern world can be felt through altered functioning of religion. The marketization of religion by religious gurus performing miracles and fascinating public, the involvement of religious organizations in the building up of hospitals and schools, working for the victims of natural disasters, etc. and politicization of religion by the outburst of fundamentalists reflect the altered character of it.

Sacred Space in Jammu Region of Jammu and Kashmir State

The Jammu and Kashmir State, which constitutes of three different regions, i.e. Jammu, Kashmir and Ladakh, has three different sub-cultures because of their own peculiar cultural heritage. The hilly tract of Jammu which reaches down to the plain land of Punjab from the south of Kashmir Valley is inhabited by '*Dogra*' of Indo-Aryan stock who profess both Hinduism and Islam (Sharma 1995). According to legends, Jammu was founded about 3000 years ago by *Jambu Lochan*, who established his rule over the area and had his capital on the left bank of the *Tawi* river. According to the understanding of historians, 'Jammu came into existence around 900 AD'. It is also about this time that the earliest references to '*Durgra Desha*' (from which the term 'Duggar' and 'Dogra' are derived and refers to Jammu region) in the form of two inscriptions on copper plates of the 11th century have been found (Wakhlu 1998). Geographically the whole of the region is divided into four major sub-divisions: The Eastern plains which include Jammu proper and erstwhile principalities of Jasrota, Balaur, Basholi, Babbur, and lower parts of Reasi and Udhampur. These plains are popularly known as *Duggar illaqa* due to the dominant *Dogra* culture prevailing here. The Western plains comprises erstwhile Bhimbar, khari-kharyali and Mirpur, which now forms part of present day Pakistan. This area was once known as Chibhal after the *Chib* clan of Rajputs. The Eastern Hills comprise Kishtwar, Bhaderwah and Dacchin areas where as the Western Hills include Rajouri, Punch and Kotli areas (Census Report of India 1911).

Commenting on the socio-economic system of the State, the Census Commissioner of J&K in his report on the census 1911 has remarked that 'The caste system in its true sense exist only in the Duggar Illaqa. Here the influence of Brahmanism has always been the strongest and there the complete hierarchy of castes and sub-caste is met with its perfection' (Gupta and Prabhakar 1988).. Geographically, Jammu region is an intermediate zone lying between plains of Punjab and ascending hills that is the tract lying between river Jhelum and river Chenab to the south of pir panjal range of mountains. A major portion of the region now forms the part of Jammu province in the State of Jammu and Kashmir. According to Raychandhari (1972), culturally Jammu region appears to have made its first contact with brahmanical culture with the arrival of *Madra* people in the region. We know that *Madra* was a section of the famous *Anu* tribe that dwelt in central Punjab and its adjoining northern region. With the coming of the *Madra*, brahmanical culture was introduced in Jammu. Since then, the brahmanical culture appears to have penetrated into all the geographical sub-regions of Jammu region depending on its acceptability. At this juncture, Jammu region in Jammu and Kashmir State (India) have its own uniqueness. Jammu city being characterized as 'city of temples' happens to be a right place for religious activities; this is evident with the presence of various holy shrines such as *Mata Vaishno Devi* Shrine, *Bhagwati Kalka* of Jammu, Sukarla temple near Billawar, Shiva temple at Sudh Mahadev near Chenani, Raghunath temple and Pirkho temple. Apart from this, the residents of the remoter parts of Jammu and especially of the hilly (*Kandi*) tracts have not only specific Gods for each village (*Granh Devata)* but every family has its own family deity/guardian God, i.e. *kul*-deity (*kul-devta* and/*kul-devi*) which they worship during their community '*maile*' congregation. On the basis of above diversified forms of religious icons, one can understand the element of sacredness in the Jammu region (see Saxena 2009b).

Dynamics of Subaltern Citizens in Jammu Region

According to S.S. Soodan (1997) the numerical strength of the depressed classes, treated as untouchable, was recorded by the Census report of 1931 as 1,70,928 person, i.e. 23.31 per cent of the entire Hindu population of the State, while in 1941, their total population in Jammu province was 1,13,422. The *Barwals* were most numerous in the Jammu and were found in Jammu province only; the *Basiths* predominated in Reasi and Mirpur districts, the *Chamar* mainly in Jammu district, the *Chura* in Poonch Jagir, the *Dhiyar* caste in all districts of Jammu province, the *Jolahas* in Reasi district only, the *Ratals* in Udhampur and Reasi and *Wattals* in Srinagar district of Kashmir.

S.D.S. Charak's (1979) work viz. *History and Culture of Himalayan States*, Vol. VIII, have explained the relatively heavy concentration of depressed classes in Jammu region. To him, it may be attributed to the fact that, here they could easily get land from Rajput and other high castes as tenant and they could earn their earnings by labour and other traditional occupations. They were not allowed to participate in social intercourse and have to suffer discrimination and untouchability. Before 1930s the condition of the SCs in the State was miserable. Narratives from the SC respondents revealed the following facts. They were not allowed to cover the upper part of their body. They could not wear turban or new clothes (especially white). During their marriages or any other occasions they were not allowed to sit on horseback and they could not hire musicians and could not go for any public procession. Those who broke these social rules had to face atrocities. They had to face discriminations in different walks of life.

Factually, high caste Hindus avoided contact with the Harijans and the touch of the Harijan obliged them to purify themselves with the bath (Census of India 1961). They were, in fact, debarred from free social intercourse. So much so, they had no access to temples and public places, like wells and tanks. Not only this, they were also denied admission to public schools. These classes had neither social status nor civic rights. The condition of this section of society was indeed pitiable (Census of India 1931, Part–I: 320–21). Having been denied the basic rights; the depressed classes were forced to lead a precarious life in isolated localities. However, Maharaja Hari Singh granted them access to temples and other public places and admission to Government schools only in 1931–32 AD.[1]

This removal of legal restrictions on the Harijans' entry in public places was probably the first in princely states of India.

The grant of this right without any strong struggle of the Harijans or absence of any public reaction against this grant by the upper castes shows the non-rigidity of untouchability and discrimination against the Harijans in this State. The removal of restrictions by the Maharaja resulted into gradual end of denial and discrimination and improvement of their social situation.

It is an established fact that historical background must have had its impact in the shaping of socio-cultural aspect of present society. The socio-religious reforms, economic gains, role of the rulers and State and other dominant agent has resulted into the flexibility in the religious practices and caste system and thus in the upliftment of Scheduled Caste population in the State (Saxena 2009a).

Socio-religious Reform Movement and the Subalterns

The socio-religious reforms in J&K have a long history. According to S.C. Sharma (1985), the proximity of Jammu to that of the Punjab helped the spread of his Arya Samaji movement in this state and a branch of the Arya Samaj was established at Jammu in 1891. In Jammu province it had branches at Mirpur, Kotli, Bhember, Rajouri, Nowshera, Reasi, Rramban, Bhaderwah, and Kishtwar.

Mainly a branch of the Arya Pratinidhi Sabha known as the 'Shuddhi Sabha' carried out the proselytization programme of the Arya Samaj. Being in constant touch with the centre of the Arya Samaj, the 'Samajist' of the Jammu and R.S. Pura tehsil did commendable work as far as proselytization among the depressed classes was concerned. Consequently, the number of Arya Samajis in the state rose to 93,944. In 1931 out of these 93,374 was in Jammu province (Census of India 1931: 290–91). Here the movement had taken a deep root particularly in Jammu and Kathua district because of the fact that these areas were situated near the Punjab border and people inhabiting these areas were highly influenced with the activities at main centre of Sialkot. Moreover, these two districts were permeated by good number of depressed class like Megh, Dooms, Chamar, and Bashiths, who easily accepted the *Shuddhi* movement to cut the shackles of untouchability. The credit for such proselytization work in the district of Kathua goes to Rambhaj Dutt of Gurdaspur. He arranged a big Shuddhi Yajna at Kathua where thousand of Harijans were given sacred thread. This raised the strength of the Arya Samaj in the district from 7,930 to 16,271 at end of 1931 (Census of India 1931: 296). In continuation with the mission, the Samaj spread education among the depressed class. It started primary schools pathshalas for depressed classes at Rehari Mohalla, R.S. Pura in Jammu district. In addition, at Garh Andral and Kal Kur Kathua district. The role played by various 'Singh Sabhas' and newspaper like 'The Ranbir' is also significant. However, it may be mentioned that the period between 1921–30 has witnessed a fierce crusade against the institution of caste. The movement against caste gained further momentum in 1931, when the *'Jat-Pat-Todak Mandal'* (organization to break caste) had been founded at Lahore and Punjab, which extended its activities to Jammu region. The most striking feature of the whole cause of social regeneration was the awakening on the part of depressed caste, which started organizing themselves with a view to demanding their due share in all lifestyles. In 1932, they submitted representation to Maharaja Hari Singh requesting for removing social evils. The first major steps that Hari Singh took in 1931 was throwing open all public educational institutions, temples and wells into public services (ibid.: 319). He also ordered that the proclamation published in the Gazette Extraordinary of the government, which later amended as any kind of obstruction to the use of public tanks, wells and so on by Harijans as a penal and cognizable offence. In 1928, a provision was made for the grant of ₹ 4000 in the form of scholarship for depressed class; fortunately, 3 'Harijan' students were there in the Prince of Wales college of Jammu during 1936–37 and 2 in 1938–39 respectively. Even the seats were reserved for their representation in local bodies and State legislature called 'Praja Sabha'. Later his wife Maharani Tara Devi (1910–67) too emphasized that all the temples should be opened to Harijan. Thus, untouchability was abolished in the State long before Mahatama Gandhi took up the same.

Role of Social Organizations in Amelioration of Weaker Sections

By the beginning of the 20th century important social and religious groups had begun forming their own organizations in Jammu province. Their efforts did have some influence in reforming the lives of the people. As pointed out in Kanchan Sharma's (1995: 54–58) work, prominent organizations directly or indirectly working for the welfare of Harijans were:

The Dogra Sadar Sabha: In order to discuss various problems of the people of this State, a meeting of about 700 notable subjects belonging to different castes and religions was convened at Jammu on 12 June 1904. In this meeting it was unanimously agreed by those present to form a body known as Dogra Sadar Sabha to promote the cause of the people and to realize their cherished desires and aspirations. This was the first public platform organized in the State to deliberate, articulate and represent the aspirations and feelings of the people to the Maharaja. Out of the various objectives of the Sadar Sabha one was the need of imparting education to lower castes and of granting liberal scholarships to students. The resolutions passed by the Sadar Sabha carried much weight with the Maharaja government since the members of the Sabha were mostly influential persons directly or indirectly associated with the government. Inclusion of the issue of education of the lower castes, i.e. Harijans as one of the objectives of the first public organization formed by the ruling elites of Jammu clearly exhibits that the denial and discrimination against the Harijans was not institutionalized.

All J&K Harijan Mandal: The first organization of the Harijans in the State was All J&K Harijan Mandal that was organized in 1920s. The leaders of the organization derived their aspirations from All India depressed castes movements, i.e. Adi-Andhra, New Bangle and Adharmi. Prominent leaders of the Mandal were Mahasha Nahar Singh, Choudhary Rangila Ram, Bhagat Chajju Ram, Mahasha Lal Chand, Mangat Ram Bhagat,

Mahasha Tui Ram, and others. The main purpose of the organization was to regain their lost social status in Hindu society particularly in Dogra Desh. In 1932 the Mandal organized a rally in which one lakh people participated. It was a non-political organization and was social in character. Main achievement of the appeals and representations of this organization was that for the first time in the history of the State of J&K the Harijans got entries into temples and schools and other public places. Gradually this organization got disintegrated. It barely remained noticeable up to 1952 and later on became redundant.

Harijan Mandal: In 1951, another organization was of the depressed castes of the State Harijan Mandal was established. This was formed on the pattern of Central Harijan Mandal. Milkhi Ram was its president. Unlike its predecessing depressed caste organization – All J&K Harijan Mandal, it was primarily a political party. It participated in the first election organized in the State on the principle of adult franchise in the year of its formation, i.e. 1951 to constitute the State's Constituent Assembly. It contested the 1951 election from 19 general seats because there was no political reservation for the depressed castes at that time. None of them were elected. In 1957 Assembly Election one of its candidates was elected to the State Legislative Assembly. The last Assembly Election that it participated was 1967. None of its candidates won in the election. As a result of not making any significant achievement in three successive elections the party started disintegrating and vanished by 1970. It got 2 per cent, 5.82 per cent and 1.89 per cent of the total polled votes in the Assembly Elections of 1951, 1957 and 1962 respectively.

From 1952–57 this organization mainly played the role of an opposition. It articulated the interests of this community and presented their demands to the government. The main demands of the party were the adoption of political, educational and job reservations in the State as it was in the rest of India. The party began an agitation on the issue of job reservation in 1952 that included organization of public meetings, dharnas and hunger strike by its leaders. As a result of this agitation the State government provided 8 per cent reservation to the depressed castes in government jobs.

Depressed Class League: All India Congress Party organized a front organization – Depressed Class League, to bring the Scheduled Castes closer to the party. A branch of the League was started in J& K in 1962. Prominent leaders of the League in J&K were Amar Nath Bhagat, Bhagat Chajju Ram, Parmanand, and others. They demanded for the provision of complete facilities to the students from the community pursuing higher studies. They further demanded for housing subsidy, land to landless tenants, reservation as per SCs population, etc. This organized functioned up to 1975.

Creation of secular social space in Jammu City:[2] It is a fact that considerable attention has been given to the development of areas based on ethnic groupings in the western cities and it is surprising that the inherent diversity of Indian urban places has not been able to prompt many studies of neighbourhood morphology (Noble and Dhussa 1982: 81). To Sharma (1993: 129–30) historicity of majority of the urban places in India and development of the distinct socio-spatial units popularly called *mohallas*, the basic morphological functional unit and basis for personal interaction and community cohesion should have provided additional impetus for such studies.

Jammu, the winter capital of Jammu and Kashmir State is an important historic centre. It has experienced phenomenal growth in the last three decades and has gained tremendous commercial, social and political significance. Its physical and population growth reflects its rising role in the regional economy, polity and culture. The city has a history of mass migrations in different times; the most recent being the influx of Kashmiri Pundits from Kashmir Valley in 1989–90. Besides, it has been receiving a slow flow of people from the surrounding region. It has traditionally been a multi-religious and multi-castes urban settlement. The 1941 census provides a pre-independence picture of social composition of the city, with the Hindus forming the largest group (60.66 per cent), followed by the Muslims (31.60 per cent), the Sikhs (4.23 per cent) and the Jains and Christian both accounting 3.49 per cent. The population of Jammu had trebled during 1901–61 from 36,130 to 1,02,738. The population almost doubled in the decade of 1971–81 from 1.40 lakh to 2.28 lakh. The 2001 Census has recorded 6,07,642 persons for the city. In 1973, the Jammu city was spread over an area of about 41.78 sq. kms. which rose to 143.6 in 1995. Till 1950, its physical spread was confined to the right bank of the river Tawi and now a equally large city has come up to its left bank. It is this part which contains some of the planned and posh localities like Gandhi Nagar, Trikuta Nagar, Channi Hamit, and Sanik colony. Other large and unplanned localities include Nanak Nagar, Sanjay Nagar, Digyana, Gangyal and Bhitindi, etc. (Figure 3). The phenomenal rapid growth in the western parts of the old city is associated with the recent migration of Kashmiri Pundits.

The density picture of the city resembles the old cities of India with the oldest parts being denser than the newer segments. The recently developed areas to the southern and western sides of the old historic centre are less dense. Slums are temporary phenomena and only found in few vacant government or private lands and house migrants from other states. The city's Master Plan, 2021 shows 3.50 hectares occupied by 7,825 squatters.

There is an intrinsic relationship between the social/ritual rank and place in a traditional Indian town. And, there is evidence to show that all over India urban places have shown conformity to this traditional pattern (Ahmed 1999: 35). The Jammu city seems no exception of this wide spread urban socio-spatial reality. The 1911 census documented the existence of separate colonies of depressed classes – *Chamars, Doms, Churas, and Meghs,* etc. on the outskirts of the city (see Figure 1 and 2). These localities were Amphalla and Rehari on the north-west and Gandu Chowni, Jogi Gate and Churia mohalla on the south. It was not the simple relationship of socially marginal social groups on the margin of the town. In addition, the inferior qualities of these localities (generally, lower elevation and steep slope) added another dimension to this unequal and hierarchical urban social space.

Figure 1

Jammu Town 1900–47

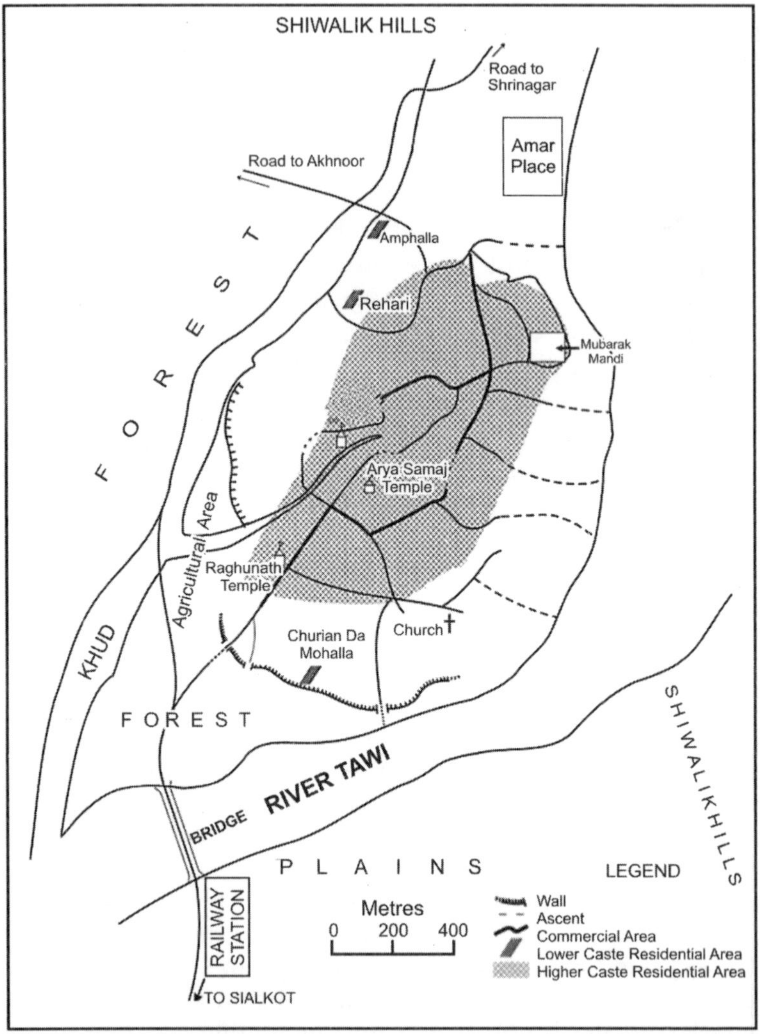

Similarly, Sharma (1993) has also reported occupation of disadvantageous sites by lower castes in some Himalayan towns in Himachal Pradesh. The roots of traditional seclusion of these groups in urban India lied in stigma conveyed by the

Figure 2

Old and New Localities of Lower Castes 1950–2010

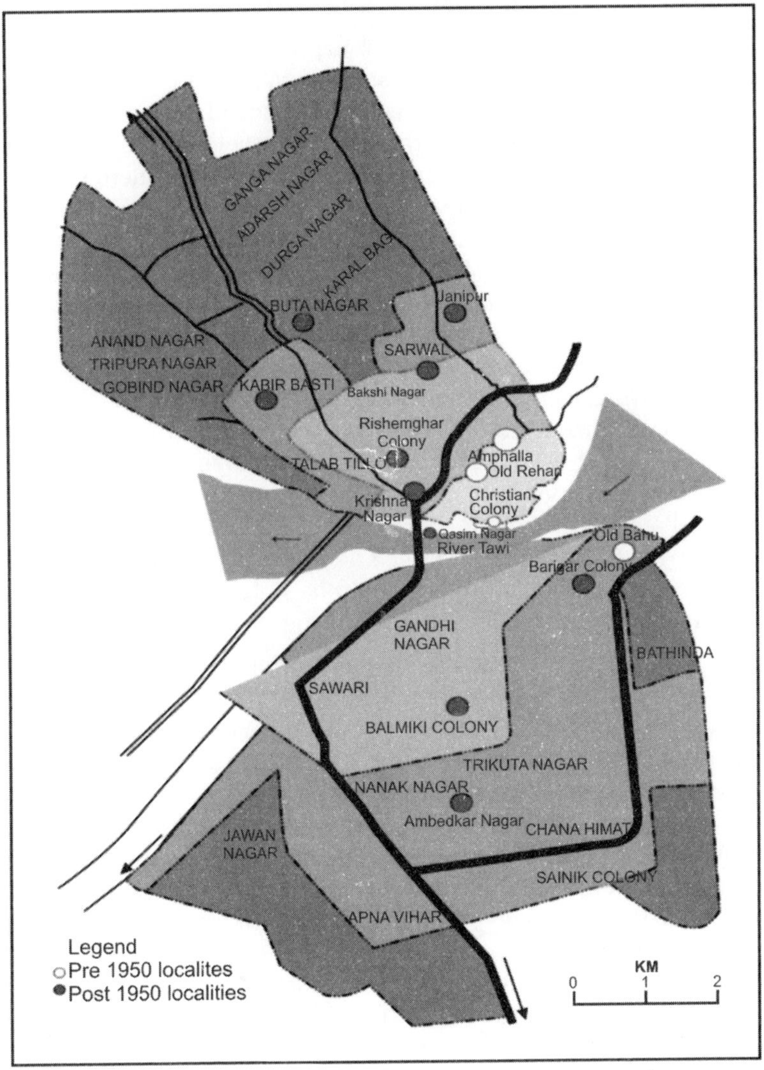

spatial association with untouchable (Duncan and Duncan 1980: 280).This traditional principle of pollution by touch or proximity shrunk their social and religious spaces of these lower castes. For example, none of the low castes, such as

Meghs, Dooms, Chamars, etc. were allowed to enter the courtyard of a Hindu temple, nor any Hindu would like to come in contact with them (Census 1901: 78).

Against the placement of the depressed castes in the urban social space and exclusionary social relationship, the area also witnessed significant initiatives both at social and government levels to bring about reforms in the social system. These reforming initiatives were part of the liberal atmosphere created by development of the democratic and political ideas and the advancement of education in the country as whole. As discussed earlier, the noteworthy influences came from the Arya Samaj Movement and Christian Missionaries. The Arya Samaj established its first branch in Jammu and Kashmir at Jammu in 1891. The role of Arya Samaj movement in the upliftment of the submerged castes is reflected in the fact that out of 1047 Aryas in Jammu and Mirpur, no less than 429 were Megh (Census Report of India 1911: 91). The Christian Missionaries opened the Alexander Missionary School in 1892.The Christian population in the state rose from 204 in 1891 to 422 in 1901. Of the total in 1910, over 202 were converts. The erstwhile Churian mohalla and now Christian colony seems to be hub of Christians in the city in pre-independence period (See Figure 2).

Another new element of expansion of secular social space has been the assertion of identity by creating symbolic religious landscapes (Figure 3). This aspect has shown a close link between social space and politic. Whelam (2002: 508) rightly suggests that where cities evolve in contentious political circumstances, aspects of the urban landscape such as political monuments, street nomenclature, buildings, city plans, and urban design initiative take on particular significance. Collectively they demonstrate the fact that the city is a product of a struggle among conflicting interests groups in search of dominion over an environment. About the contested space an illustrations is as follows – Buta Nagar, a small locality in the west Jammu was named after a venerated old community member of the lower caste group in 1980s. A banner was put up at the main entrance in presence of a local political leader. In 1990s, this locality experienced rapid growth due to migration of Kashmir Pandits and other migration. A group of new inhabitants made several attempts to give new

Figure 3

Prominent Religious Places 2010

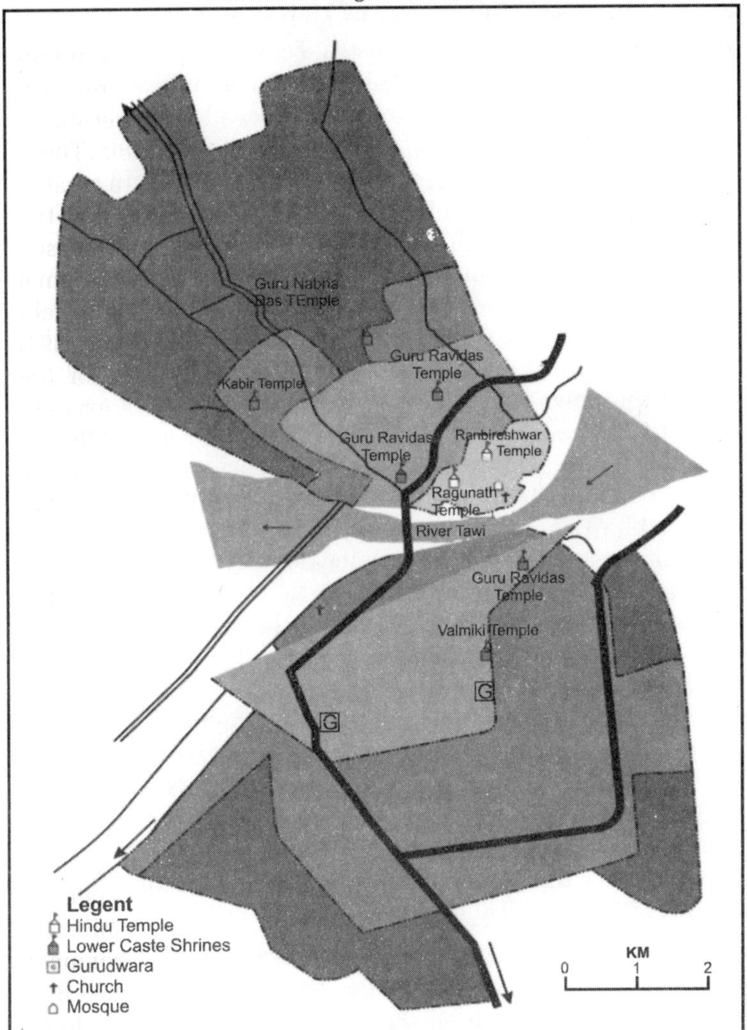

name to the locality. They removed the old banner and put another banner with new name. The conflict about identification of space persisted for few days and finally resolved in favour of lower caste Hindus with the intervention of local authorities and local political leaders (Raj 2003).

Emerging religious space for weaker sections in Jammu city

One finds temple-based religious activities are the most exciting; it is no exaggeration to characterize temples as the motor of popular religious revivals. Temples typically sponsor and stage a wide range of folk cultural activities, including performances by folk dance troupes, musical bands and story-tellers, folk opera, offering presentation processions, animal sacrifices, temple festivals, and so forth. Besides being a site of both individual and communal worship, a temple is also a political, economic, and symbolic resource and a generator of such resources. A beautifully built temple and a well attended temple festival attest not only to the efficacy of the deity but also to the organizational ability of the temple association and the community. The lower caste Hindus of the Jammu city has evolved their own religious spaces on the lines of higher castes. They have constructed temples of saints and reformers belonging to the lower caste Hindus. The prominent temple includes Valmiki temple, Kabir temple, Guru Ravi Das temple, Guru Nabha Das, and others (see Figure 3). It is interesting to note that most of the temples are located in the heart of the city. They are in the posh localities with huge areas and made marvelously (see Figure 4). Normally the sacred space is used by the Scheduled Castes of Jammu region that come together for the celebration of birth anniversaries and 'shobha yatra' of great persons of their community. Religious congregations, processions and celebration of anniversaries or '*prakash divas*' of the personalities like Ambedkar, Ravi Dass, Kabir, Nabha Das, and others are significant because this collectivity and its demonstration is in public sphere i.e. the main city area and they are allowed now without any obstacles and also sometimes with the support of few political leaders.

The formation of community organizations has been another prominent religious practice in the city. These politico-religious institutions, emulated from the high castes, have been used as platform for assertion and development of new identities at macro-level. For example, merging of Megh Sabha into Kabir/Bhagat Sabha, and so called Chamar Sabha into Guru Ravi Dass Sabha. And, this new mergence has given rise to the political mobilization and assertion through annual processions in the

Figure 4

Guru Ravi Dass Temple at prime location in Jammu city

memory of the prominent iconic figures of the downtrodden community.[3] These processions are perceived by the communities as means to enhance the political visibility and identity assertion of the community. Besides, it is also perceived as the reflection of freedom for the social space. Viewing urban social space in this sense, one finds it as becoming more contested, fragmented and attained more complexity.

In conclusion, the above deliberations and exemplifications reflect the creation of religious spaces and also the lower caste Hindu identity assertion through these places. Population growth and territorial expansion of Scheduled Castes in Jammu city is indicative of their emerging new localities in urban sphere. One may deduce that historically, the so called scheduled castes were residing in the periphery of Jammu town but with the gradual pace of urbanization they have become part of the main city. One can infer the spatial mobility of the weaker sections in terms of their proximity to the main city. Few localities like Valmiki colony, Kabir Nagar, Krishna nagar, Talab Khatika, etc.

are heartland of the Jammu city and are dominated by the inhabitation of weaker section. Although government had rehabilitated them in separate colonies, and which unintentionally segregate them from the mainstream localities. However, the modern forces and the pace of urbanization had diluted the airtight compartmentalized segregation of the weaker section and paved them way for secular living with the other high caste groups. It had not only brought democratic dwelling space but also provided them dignity with the new level of assertion. Needless to mention that the new governmental and civil society initiatives too are also resulting into the erection of new monuments, temples, buildings, memorials, and statues symbolizing their identity and assertion. Collective socio-religious gatherings and congregations in these spaces reflects high level of mobilization and assertion among the weaker sections belonging to Jammu city and its surroundings.

Notes

1. Fortnightly Reports of the Resident of Kashmir for the first half of September 1930, GoI, P.D.F. No. 22-P (sec) of 1930, Crowns film A.C.C. No. 291, (N.A.I), p. 24. A brief note on the administration of the Jammu and Kashmir for the year 1932, J&K Government Publication, p. 10; Government J&K, Vol. 4, No. 4, April, 1947, p. 3.
2. For further details, see 'Urban Social Space and Weaker Sections: A Case Study of Jammu City', Dr Ambedkar Studies Centre, University of Jammu (jointly with Dr Devinder Singh, Department of Geography), 2010.
3. Ibid.

References

Ahmed, Aijazuddin, 1999, *Social Geography*, Rawat Publications, Jaipur and New Delhi.

Census Report of India, 1911, Government of India, Jammu and Kashmir.

Charak, S.D.S, 1979, *History and Culture of Himalayan States*, Vol. VIII, Light and Life Publishers, Delhi, p. 13.

Chidester, D. and E.T. Linenthal (eds), 1995, *American Sacred Space*, Indiana University Press, Bloomington, IN.

Deffontaines, P., 1953, 'The Religious Factor in Human Geography', *Diogenes*, Vol. 1, No. 2.

Duncan, James S. and Nancy G. Duncan, 1980, 'Residential Landscapes and Social Worlds: A Case Study of Hyderabad, Andhra Pradesh', in David E. Sopher (ed.), *An Exploration of India: Geographical Perspectives on Society and Culture*, Cornell University Press, New York.

Fenn, Richard K. (ed.) 2001, *Sociology of Religion*, Blackwell Publishing Ltd., UK.

Gupta, N.S. and N.C. Prabhakar, 1988, *Socio-Economic Development of J&K*, Jay Kay Book House, Jammu.

Habermas, J., 1988, *Post-Metaphysical Thinking*, Polity Press, Cambridge.

Haynes, Jeff, 1997, 'Religion, Secularisation and Politics: A Postmodern Conspectus', *Third World Quarterly*, Vol. 18, No. 4, September.

Isaac, E., 1963, 'Myths, Cults and Livestock', *Diogenes*, Vol. 41.

Jevtic, Miroljub, 2007, 'Political Science and Religion, *Politics and Religion Journal*, Vol. 1, No. 1.

——, 2008, 'Religion and Relations between Genders', *Politics and Religion Journal*, Vol. 2, No. 1.

Kong, L., 2001, 'Mapping "New" Geographies of Religion: Politics and Poetics in Modernity', *Progress in Human Geography*, Vol. 25, No. 2.

Kothari, Rajni, 1970, *Politics in India*, Orient Longman, New Delhi.

Kurtz, L., 1995, *Gods in the Global Village: The World's Religions in Sociological Perspective*, Pine Forge Press, Thousand Oaks, CA.

Levine, G.J., 1986, 'On the Geography of Religion', *Transactions of the Institute of British Geographers*, New Series, Vol. 11, No. 4.

Noble, Allen G. and Ramesh Dhussa, 1982, 'Ethnic Neighbourhoods in Indian Cities: The Paras of Dumka and the Bengali Tola of Bhagalpur', in Allen G. Noble and Ashok K. Dutt (eds), *India: Cultural Patterns and Processes*, Westview Press, Colorado.

Pernau, Margrit, 2005, 'Multiple Identities and Communities: Re-Conceptualizing Religion', in Jamal Malik and Helmut Reifeld (eds), *Religion Pluralism in South Asia and Europe*, OUP, UK.

Portier, Philippe, 2011, 'Religion and Democracy in the Thought of Jürgen Habermas', *Springer Science and Business Media, LLC*, Vol. 48, No. 5.

Raj, Mulkh, 2003, 'Local Community Leader', Interview by Authors, Buta Nagar, Jammu, 14 March.

Raychandhari, H.C., 1972, *Political History of Ancient India*, University of Calcutta Press, Calcutta.

Saxena, Ashish, 2009a, *Shifting Manifestations: Scheduled Castes in Jammu and Kashmir*, Saksham Books International, Jammu.

——, 2009b, 'Religion, Caste and Community: Identity Substantiation through "Maile" Congregations among the Dogras of Jammu and Kashmir', *Politics and Religion*, Vol. III, No. 1.

Sharma, K.D., 1993, 'Social Morphology of Himalayan Towns', in Aijazuddin Ahmed (ed.), *Social Structure and Regional Development: A Social Geography Perspective*, Rawat Publications, Jaipur.

Sharma, Kanchan, 1995, *Socio-Political Aspiration of J&K People*, Akshay Publisher, Jammu.

Sharma, S.C., 1985, 'Socio-Religious Activities of the Arya Samaj in J&K State', *Maharshi Dayanand University Research Journal*, Vol. 3, No. 2, October.

Smith, D.M., 1999, 'Geography, Community and Morality', *Environment and Planning A*, Vol. 31.

Soodan, S.S., 1997, *Jammu under the Reign of Maharaja Hari Singh*, Vinod Publications, Jammu, p. 47.

Sopher, D., 1967, *Geography of Religions*, Prentice Hall, Englewood Cliffs, NJ.

Wakhlu, Somnath, 1998, *The Rich Heritage of J&K: Studies in Art, Architecture, History and Culture of the Region*, Gyan Publishing House, New Delhi.

Whelam, Y., 2002, 'The Construction and Deconstruction of a Colonial Landscape: Monuments to British Monarchs in Dublin Before and After Independence', *Journal of Historical Geography*, Vol. 28, No. 4.

Young, I.M., 1990a, 'The Ideal of Community and the Politics of Difference', in L.J. Nicholson (ed.), *Feminism/Postmodernism*, Routledge, London, pp. 300–23.

——, 1990b, *Justice and the Politics of Difference*, Princeton University Press, Princeton, NJ.

5

Buddhist Identity

A Case Study of Buddhist Women's Narratives in Nagpur City

Ajay I. Choudhary

It has been said that the history of ancient India is nothing but the conflict between Buddhism and Brahmanism. It means that Karl Marx's philosophy of conflict is still relevant to be observed as a tool of social change. The social change occur in society at different level; firstly by targeting individual for change at limited sphere without touching system, secondly individual transformation in his behaviour with specific context, example of religious movements. While other change could be observed in the context of revolution or transformation in which people are not interested to work within system rather they feel that the system itself has problems of values and morals that could not rectified at all and over through it applying any means. At the present scenario, the institution has become major centres for expecting social change in India either through political or social institution.

The social changes gradually started in India either to reform its society or to change the social system itself. Those who fail to rectify the notion of caste system within Hinduism like Dr B.R. Ambedkar, Ayoti Tass, Laxmi Narsu have taken alternative step to reclaim the lost self-respect and humanism which was existed in Buddhism. The leaders like him interpreted and explored lost dignity and pride of untouchable in Buddhism by presenting them the lost history from subaltern point of view. It has created the wave of consciousness and courage to question the faith in Hinduism. As a result of it, the Mahar and other untouchables Community embraced the Buddhism under the leadership of Dr B.R. Ambedkar on 14 October 1956. The reason behind of embracing Buddhism could locate into three folds that is Buddhism is an aboriginal religion of India and ex-untouchables as well as touchable were none other than Buddhists. Secondly, Buddhism is based on the rationality with scientific approach. In other words, Buddhism is not based on science rather science is based on Buddhism. Thirdly, Buddhism has universal principles which has been inculcated in Indian constitution that is liberty, equality and fraternity with social justice. Thus, by quoting Richards Taylor's, it makes point that there is very much similarity between Constitution and Buddhism to express the religious and political life of the community (Viswanathan 1998: 228). It might be the vision of Ambedkar that this universal principle would be the solution to Indian caste based society. In the Indian caste based society, fraternity is more imperative step for cementing the different castes of Indian society. Therefore, in his posthumous writing of Buddha and His Dhamma, are carefully recognized to fall into symmetrical parts covering not only the conversion of sinful people like Brahmins, criminals and other fallen beings but also conversion of women and oppressed social classes (ibid.: 229).

While embracing Buddhism, Ambedkar has given 22 vows so that the common man of Buddhist community could follow the Buddhism at his/her simplest manner. He did not want any yardstick to become Buddhist or Buddhist monk. According to him, anyone who will follow the 22 vows is the Buddhists. At the present circumstance, it has been said that due to Buddhism, the untouchable community like Mahar observed the drastic transformation in their lifestyle. Now they are leading in every sector of life either political or social. In this regards, the acute riddle arise that at what extend the Buddhism has changed the life of Buddhist women. Whether the

Buddhism has really created any impact on them or still they are treated with same caste mind as a lower or untouchable despite their formation of new entity. It is well known fact that this Mahar community embraced Buddhism to liberate themselves from Hindu social order but they are struck with old caste identities and recognizing with new identity from different point of views.

The reason behind to examine the narrative is to explore the meaning carried by the people about their life and grasp highly expressive cultural elements exist in narratives. It has stated that a narrative is beginning and ending a fact by distinguishing it from the rest of world and opposes it to real world (Mcquillan 2000: 88). The individual experience has the meaning which could figure out from the past experiences. Therefore, providing the account of own stories is nothing but a reflection of own identity. In this process, an individual recognize him/herself in their narratives and we seek to comprehend human events, action and account to make sense in the form of narratives or stories (Issac Venema 2000: 117). It is not what happened to their life rather what meaning they carry while experiencing their lives. It is nothing but to subjectify the meaning while objectifying the reality. The meaning could be grasping through the conduct of human behaviour or action because in every action there is intension and without intension the meaning is meaningless. For this, I have analysed the narrative given by the Buddhist women about their understanding of new identity, i.e. Buddhists identity.

Impact of Education on Buddhist Women

Many studies has been conducted on the neo-Buddhists community on their development and socio-economic progress but all this studies are centred around the male point view and unable to provide the accountability of women perception which is the major part of Buddhist community. It is mentioned that perception of Buddhist has changed after the conversion. According to this study, Buddhist women carrying two perception where one is conversant with and inspired by Dr Ambedkar's thought while other one totally unaware about it which is useful for understanding the issues of consolidation of organization and unity (Paswan 2002: 202) which is similar to my study. Therefore, I have divided the Buddhists women into two parts; firstly to understand the Buddhist women who are following the Ambedkar's principles and secondly those who are still not acquaint with Ambedkar's philosophy of Buddhism. Hence, the historical intelligible of Buddhist conversion could be phenomenologizes by analysing the narratives of Buddhist women. It focuses the objectification of meaning in the context of Buddhist conversion which would reflect the consciousness about the Buddhist conversion under the leadership of Ambedkar. It has been observed that Buddhist women perceived the Buddhist conversion in the arena of caste system and feel that worshipping Hindu God doesn't have place in their home and it has happened due to the education. Supriya, a married and post-graduate student of Pali, explains explicitly about the progress in Buddhist women due to Buddhism and education. She said:

> There is change in Buddhist women due to emancipation from caste system and more opportunity of upward mobility to avail education. I got consciousness because of my father and some movies like Dr Baba Saheb Ambedkar about the condition of my people.

It means that conversion has benefited them and provided opportunity to advance them in the domain of education. Historically the women does not have place in education system. The code of Manu law has restricted the women to right to have education. It is well known aspect that education leads to think and ask to behave rationally. Prapti, working in Central Bank of India explains that it is the impact of constitutional rights which was denied by the Manu constitution. It has been observed that Buddhism has considered being caste due to caste certificate in which the neo-Buddhist has to mention their caste. Although, the caste is not at all exit theologically but might be practiced by them:

> There is change in Buddhist women due to educational opportunity which was denied by the constitution of manusmriti

> but the present constitution has granted the equal rights and right to education to us. For me Buddhism is not caste and any one can follow it. It is very pity that Buddhist women doesn't know about the Buddhism and even devoid of having the knowledge about Buddhists conversion under the leadership of Dr B.R. Ambedkar.

There is no doubt that the education has changed their thinking and become conscious about their constitutional rights which has assisted to open the door of progress. There might be thinking of Dr Ambedkar that education could lead to create casteless society. It could tantalize on the individual's perception that in what way it has been engaged whether to maintain the caste or annihilate the caste. The main impact of Buddhist conversion is education. For Disha, a civil engineer, it has happened due to education.

> The education has changed the thinking process of Buddhist women especially the educated women but the uneducated women is still dependent on other and feel weak. Now educated women can inculcate the culture in the right direction and can play her major role in every direction of development like in economic, culture and social.

The change in Buddhist women doesn't occur only due to Buddhist conversion. It could be seen merely the impact on the first or second generation of Buddhist community but the third generation become more enthusiastic after knowing about the Ambedkarism's ideological dimension of social change on the basis of universal principles that is liberty, equality and fraternity. The rationality of Buddhism dispenses the space to question the existing social order which is not allowing them to live with dignity. Hence, the Buddhist women after becoming conscious about their own history worked in the different Buddhist or Ambedkarite organization. The subhangi katekar administer the account that 'Buddhist women which are working in different Ambedkarite organization are more independent and free to take their decision as compare to inactive Buddhists women'.

> I became conscious due to Buddhist organization and developed my personality. As a result of it, I am no more dependent on others and can take decision which is applicable to my consciousness. I have observed that women working for society are no more dependent on others at all.

It is creditable that change in Buddhist women is due to accepting the Buddhist principles. The Buddhist principle of equality is inculcated in the thoughts of their family members. The educational consciousness has penetrated into the mind of Buddhist women due to Ambedkar's message of Educate, Agitate and Organize. The message implies to individual consciousness in which an individual not only has to educate himself but also about the society. While educating himself, the individual would come across ideas which may not be applicable to the concept of universal principles, i.e. equality, liberty and fraternity would agitate and after arriving on issues of humanism would lead to organizing the society. In the Buddhist community, the mutation in their life honorary to education but the others aspects has not materialized practically. It shows that Buddhists community has given more emphasis on education. In this regards, the Kalpana Meshram, an Architect, explicit that Buddhist women lead in education due to the Ambedkar's message of Educate, Agitate and Organize.

> Buddhist women are leading in education due to the Ambedkar message of Educate, Agitate and Organize. Education has created impact on our life. Even in poor family, women have given more important to education which is the main reason for transforming the life of Buddhist women. She has developed very speedily compare to other women (Non-Buddhist) of society.

It has been observed that in Buddhist community explicitly availing the space to question the traditional aspects of Buddhism like paritaran pat (rituals done before to enter in newly made house), superstition exist in Buddhism and Hinduism and also to patriarchal values. According to them, it is only religion which allows questioning every aspects of reality with rationality. Conversion to Buddhism has transit their life and able to shed the feeling of inferiority complex. In other words, the Usha Jambulkar, M.Sc (Zoology), B.Ed and working teacher, focus the broader aspects of conversion in the reference to caste system of Hindu religion.

> We have to gain the confidence and wipe out the inferiority complex being part of caste system after the conversion. I feel more confident and pride. I don't feel that I am inferior to any so called upper castes nor to men of our community. This change occurs in our life due to conversion and three words Educate, Agitate and Organize given by Ambedkar. As a result, it has developed the healthy atmosphere of education and struggle against unequal system of Indian society. Due to education and awareness, we are not getting into Hindu religion and nor involved into superstition. We have feeling of equality.

But the inquisition arises that change in Buddhist women could not locate complete transformation in their life. It has been said that Buddhism is based on practice and merely conversion is not enough to claim themselves as Buddhists until each individual of community would not follow the path of 22 vows given by Dr Ambedkar.

After fifty decades of conversion, Mahar community usually recognized as Buddhist on government records but in practice it is difficult to categorize them as Buddhist. The reason behind it is a perplexity of inter-relationship between Buddhism and Hinduism. Palavi Nandeshwar, civil engineer, has shifted the responsibility on educated people which has not played role for annihilating the caste system due to devoid of knowledge about Buddhism. Thus, they remain aloof from Buddhism and still attach with the notion of Hinduism.

> This has happened because of unaware about the Buddhist history and don't know about the basic aspects of Buddhism. It is not clear to my community. I feel that role and responsibility of educated people to propagated Buddhism in right direction has not played properly. As a result of it, there is lot of puzzle among Buddhist community. If we get the awareness of Buddhism and spread it with right direction, I

feel, our people would not feel hesitate and reluctant to reveal their Buddhist identity.

Thus, the transfiguration in Buddhist women is abided with reference to leaving Hinduism. It has visualized that the definition of change has limited to worshipping and celebrating Hindu festivals. It clarifies that Buddhist women are superstitious due to influence of Hinduism but those who followed and read Ambedkar has different picture of Indian history and Buddhism itself. The question of investigation has raised by the Buddhist women itself that there are people who worship both religion by keeping Hindu God and Goddess picture along with Ambedkar and Buddha's idol. If any would oppose this particular action would often replied on the name of orthodox Buddhist. This understanding raise the issue whether Buddhist are opposing the teaching of Buddha or not been trustworthy to Ambedkar itself.

Politics of Festivals

It is perceived that the Mahar community left all the Hindu god and goddess by adopting 22 vows given by Dr Ambedkar in which it has mentioned that mahars would not celebrate and worship any Hindu God and Goddess and follow the panchsheel of Buddha. The idea and reason behind the conversion has passed out from grandfather or father to their children. This new generation and old generation have their own intelligible about this conversion. It occurs due to oppressive system of caste and for some it is to negate the religion of inequality and establish the Buddhism on the basis of rationality.

After the fifty decades of conversion, the Buddhism has been perceived by the Buddhist community at different level. It is overtly observed two religious ideologies at equal platform by celebrating their festivals without differentiating them because fusion exist in their relationship between Buddhism and Hinduism (Shastree 1996: 73–74). Thus, it is surprising to know that people of Buddhist community is popularly proceeding the both religious ideologies which is in very contradictory to each other. It is unadjustable to represent the ideas of equality and inequality at the same platform. The Hindu festivals like diwali, dushhara, holi, etc. are not only the symbolic representation of domination of Hindu culture but also perpetuate the principles of inequality on the name of equality principles which goes against the Buddhism and Phule-Ambedkar understanding. It is not that Buddhist are celebrating only Hindu festivals but also Buddhist festivals by keeping portrait of Buddha and Ambedkar. They celebrate Buddhist festivals like birthday of Ambedkar, i.e. 14 April, ashokdushami (14 October) and Buddha Poornima. Thus, it is enthusiastic to capture the perception of Buddhist women in domain of conversion and 22 vows. It has observed that people are following both traditions that are old and new at the same time by providing their own reasons. One of the respondents Supriya speaks what Buddha and Babasaheb said, teaching provided by her father. She speaks that how her Buddhist friends celebrate and invite her for Hindu festivals.

> My Buddhist friends celebrate all Hindu festivals like Navratra, Gauri Puja, Diwali and all Hindu festivals. My father has told to follow what Baba Saheb and Buddha have said. I feel if it is not in my culture why I should follow. I don't have any restriction to follow Hindu culture and Ambedkar hasn't done only for SC's but he has done for all community. It is different things the people has not take cognizance of his contribution.

The other side of viewpoint is that just negating the Hindu culture and tradition would not make themselves as a Buddhists. It has emphasized that the principles of Buddhism is based on practice and rationality. If it is follow, than it is complicated to claim as Buddhist. It always struck to non-Buddhists world that despite having guidance of Buddhism, why there is commonality between Buddhist people and Hindu people. For this, people belonging to Phule-Ambedkarite ideology resist to celebrate festivals and follow the Hindu Culture but who are untouched to ideas of Phule-Ambedkar are still roaming around old tradition of Hinduism. It has been argued that converted Buddhist people in fact belong to Hinduism. Thus, it is not easy to separate them from their old identity. Hence, it makes to think that the Buddhist community are deceiving the Ambedkar and his teaching or inferiority complex make them to behave in such manner. Kirti, working girl in Punjab National Bank focus the broader aspects of Buddhist Community and question the action of Buddhist women itself.

> If we follow Buddhism, we can create separate identity which is yet to form ... whatever the changes has taken place in the life of Buddhist women only due to the efforts of Baba Saheb Ambedkar. If Babasaheb has said something we must have to follow because he has provided the reasons and rationality to understand it. He is Guru to us, if Guru's Guru (Buddha) is saying something, it must have logic. Now people are moving to that direction which has been opposed by Ambedkar. His wish was that they should not follow Hindu religion based on caste system or superstition. He has studied in great Universities of the world and given us Buddhism after studying all religion. Even after this, people do not trust him, what a disappointment and shame to our community!!. If he could wish, he would have taken Mahayana or Hinyana but he has taken only Buddhism so that it could reach to common understanding of people. In spite of taking all facilitates, if people are not paying back to society and not following Buddhism, it means that they are deceiving Babasaheb ... they usually do the puja of Gautama Buddha and Babasaheb but never do the puja in the direction of panchsheela and astan marg along with her children.

It is realized that youth of Buddhist community expecting the change within community in the direction of what Ambedkar said to them. The celebration of Buddhist festivals now has changed. It has been argued that the Buddhist celebration is not restricted to only dancing or just distributing sweets among the people but now the people at the contemporary epoch are moving towards organizing such programmes in which an individual could enhance his/her capacity to know about Buddhism and thoughts against system of slavery. For it, Disha, a civil engineer unfold the changing activities taking place in

Buddhist community and question just following Buddhism without thinking is not make any difference to other religion.

> Now days, Buddhist people organizing seminars, speeches and debates related to Phule-Ambedkar and Buddhism which is new trend in our society. I feel that some years back people for the sake of going, they were going to vihars and doing vandana which was celebration for them. I have observed and seen last two years there is group discussion. Women's participation is always in large numbers at Buddhist celebration. Just following rituals of Buddhism is not but following Hinduism. If you are following Buddhists thoughts is Buddhist. If Buddhist are following both culture (Hinduism and Buddhism) cannot be said as Buddhist.

It is well-known fact that Ambedkar has denied refugees to sangha as he said that present monk are not capable to conduct his behaviour on the basis of morals and according to principles of Buddhism. There might be a reason that Buddhist community could not produce the Buddhist monk who could be conscious about Buddhist values and become the light of knowledge for Buddhist community. As a result of it, the Buddhist community become paralysed due to lack of enlightened Buddhist monk which make them understand the modern principles of Buddhism on the basis of science. It is historically proved that the lack of Buddhist laity has become one of the reason for the decline of Buddhism in ancient India. Even without the monk guidance people still celebrate Buddhist festivals according to their own knowledge. The respondent Kalpana Meshram, an architect, provide mix account of festivals they celebrate in their home which seems to disorientation in her perception.

> There is lack of awareness in those who perform Hindu rituals. It is because the Buddhist monk has not worked for the propagation of Buddhism. We don't celebrate any Hindu festivals which exist in my family. But sometime we prepare some sweets and fire crackers in our family. But I feel when I read and understand these things, gradually this type of celebration cease to celebrate. If we are not doing these things doesn't mean that we celebrate Hindu festivals ... we just have

> to propagate our own religion without hurting anyone's feeling. In short we should practice our religion rather one speaking about others.

The statement seems to be defensive regarding the celebration and distributing the sweets on the occasion of Hindu festivals. This is ergo it is unable to make remarks that whatever the notion they celebrate the Hindu festivals or participate, it is indirectly supporting the Hindu festivals only by saying that our notion of celebration is different to what Hindu perceived or celebrate it. The other phenomena exist in Buddhist community is that they endeavour to negate all Hindu tradition but celebrate anyone of the Hindu festivals by giving their own reason or general perception of society. Usha Jambulkar expresses her comprehension and justification about celebration of Buddhist festivals in relation Hindu festivals.

> I don't know much about other festivals and the purpose of their celebration. I use to celebrate Diwali because of my children. I feel Diwali is festival of everyone and because of it the feeling of sarvadharam sadbhav. I felt why we should not celebrate diwali during 14th April or day of Dhamma Chakra Parivartan Din.

It seems that Buddhist people trying to replace the same tradition of Hindu festivals on the days of Buddhist festivals which is nothing but transferring the Hindu tradition on the name of Buddhist festivals of 14 April or 14 October. Although, the Buddhist community people denied the celebration of Hindu festivals or tradition of inequality exist in social system but at the same time they participate in close friends function or Hindu festivals. Being close friends, it is difficult to deny them and if they would agitate on such issues, would spoil their social relationship and remain stuck forever. In return, Buddhist women would not call them for their Buddhist celebration. Vibha Gajbhiye, an financial advisor of LIC, visualizes the pressure of their close surrounding and actively participates in social issues and regularly visit to dikshabhoomi of Nagpur.

> We go to participate in Hindu festivals in very selective places like our close friends. They involve us in their family programmes with respect and speak very respectfully. I feel that as a friend there is nothing wrong to participate because they are our close friends. I have friends like Brahmins, Punjabi which won't call us on such occasion but other occasion like birthday or get-together we participate to maintain our relationship. We don't call any non-Buddhist people as we don't make any sweets nor we called them in our house ... we celebrate all Buddhist festivals and regularly visit dikshabhoomi and conduct medical camps for people who visit on Dhamma Diksha Day.

The other aspects of Buddhist women's perception towards festivals of Hindu and Buddhism internalize it while communicating and inviting non-Buddhist people in her religious festivals. The reason behind to celebrate Hindu festivals is rooted in their inferiority complex and frightens to question or denied their religious authority. It is surprising that Buddhist wants to maintain their relationship at their self-respect but this phenomenon is not seen and applicable to know Buddhist people. It is not that Buddhist women never resist but at very minute way and sometimes have to follow their Hindu religious god and goddess for sake of their happiness or feel good factor. In this regards, respondent Dharmapala Pakidey, housewife, explicitly express the relationship between Buddhist and non-Buddhist.

> We don't celebrate any Hindu festivals rather we celebrate Buddha jayanti, Ambedkar jayanti and Buddha Pornima. In our celebration, we call others community people like Brahmins, Maratha, Kunbi in our colony. Very few come like Brahmins but when they call us we won't go for any Hindu festivals. Sometimes I go for haldi Kunko (celebration of opening ceremonies) but unwillingly. They sometime ask us to take namaskar of their deity which I don't like and that's why I try to avoid their home visit on such occasion. I feel that bowing to Hindu deity means we go to his/her refugees which I don't want to do it. They might be feeling bad but whenever they ask me why I don't come to their festivals!! I tell them

> that we have taken oath of not worshipping Hindu God and Goddess. They use to feel surprise of my act by saying that the Buddhist from my community follow Hinduism than why not you? I say that those who follow only Buddhism is Buddhist and those who don't follow are not Buddhist at all.

It is also internalized by the Buddhist women that whatever they are doing is going against the values of Buddhism and Ambedkar's teaching. It might be matter of minority and majority. It has been captured that where the population in some areas of Nagpur is less compare to non-Buddhist people like Hindus. The experience of Buddhist people reflect the pressure and inferiority complex in their thoughts of performing tradition of Hindu culture. They agree that they are feeling contradiction while celebrating Hindu festivals which don't have place in their everyday life, despite having participation of upper caste and lower caste in every festival. The Sobha Suryawanshi, housewife, explain the same sight of thoughts while responding the perception of celebrating the Hindu and Buddhists festivals.

> We celebrate all festivals. We have to do it because we have to live with other castes people in their areas and to maintain our relation we have to do it which is not applicable to our consciousness. We call them in our festivals and we also go to their festivals. Sometime I feel it is contradictory to my consciousness but we involved with them in their festivals just as fun and they insist us to come and we have to go as don't have choice. I feel we haven't become Buddhist the way we want to become.

Other side of picture speaks with very positive hope and more concerned about her community. It seems that some Buddhist women do not bother about the relationship. The reasons behind is that they are having their own Buddhist community people in large number and other community people less in quantity. Sureka Suryawansi produce positive hope of negating Hindu culture based on inequality and people would follow the Buddhism on the basis of rationality.

> Our religion is based on rationality and more emphasis on reason. If it is suitable to your logic, than you should follow it

> or leave it. It is based on science and one should practice it. The gradual change occurring in women, it is because of involvement of women in Buddhism. We celebrate our Ambedkar jayanti just like diwali. We accept the sweets of diwali occasion but never participate in their festivals. When our celebrations come we use to give sweets to other community in same way. If we won't participate in Hindu religion festivals, it never disturbed my relation with other community members. I feel that if I would follow my religion properly, than my community people will also follow in the same way. Thus, there is need to create good example before my community.

It confirms that a Buddhist woman could maintain social relationship without compromising her Buddhist identity. Historically, the isolation and exclusion has resisted the different castes to communicate with each other. As a result of it, the cleavage in communication created confusion and misunderstanding in society. The present era has diluted the feeling of isolation and sharing the values of culture without disturbing social relation exist in society.

Politics of Equality and Patriarchy

Women of Buddhist community have acquired new identity as Buddhist after the conversion. At the time of conversion, Ambedkar has explained reasons behind conversion and provided 22 vows which explain basic tenets of Buddhist philosophy for common man and women to follow it. It was Ambedkar's understanding that without active participation of women in any social movement would not make it successful. It has been said that women in Ambedkarite movement could contextualize into three aspects that is role in Ambedkarite movement which is yet to studied in direction of their contribution in movement, participation and responsibility in movement, and economic empowerment of Dalit women (Paswan 2002: 204). Thus, the question rose that men of Buddhist Buddhism is not only to focus on rationality but also emphasis is on universal principles essential for human being. If we analysed the concept of equality in the context of Buddhist community, it has been noticed that Buddhists men are preferably less patriarchal compared to other non-Buddhist men. It has been said that patriarchy in Buddhist men is gradually getting wipe out due to Buddhist humanistic principles of equality. In what sense, the dominance and unequal power relation between men and women perpetuated is unexplored aspect of Buddhist community. The patriarchy prevents women in every sphere of life like decision-making position, under representation in premier state institution and imposes violence on them. The story of patriarchy in Buddhist women's perception explains patriarchy differently. In this regards, Sarika, M.A in Pali literature situate patriarchy at liberal position and make an agreement that male wishes to give equal opportunity to female but resist their male ego.

> I feel men of Buddhist community are not much liberal but want to keep her under control. They think that giving more liberty would hurt their dominance and status. They want to give equality in walk of life but male ego resists them. But nowadays, some men are really giving the opportunity to their wife but the percentage of such persons are very less.

The above expression also unfold the understanding that liberal atmosphere also remain in the hand of male. In other words, sometime male become the deciding factors on the behalf of female. It means that concept of liberty has been understood by men but the same concept has narrowed down for women which is nothing but patriarchy notion. The expectation and hope of Buddhist women has related to Buddhism itself and expecting that male approach would transform towards women when men would grasp Buddhism outlook on the basis of equality. Kirti, explains the two categories of men existing in Buddhist community.

> In Buddhist community, the men have developed themselves speedily compared to women. It has been happening because of long patriarchy values carried by Buddhist men which is not part of Buddhism. It is not that all men are doing and behaving in the domain of patriarchy but some are having liberal attitude and behavior towards the women. Those who

> don't have such approach are devoid of Buddhism and nor are they Buddhists at least in the level of equality. In this context, we cannot be Buddhist, if our women and girls are not enjoying liberty and equality. Such a mentality is superficial where they speak and lecture on the liberation of women emancipation but practically they are not doing.

Thus, it is matter of validity attached to Buddhist men's on practice and theory. The theory of justice percolates in Buddhist community, on other hand they won't allow provide space to their women the way they acquire. This type of notion existed in Buddhist community because men are not enlightened nor conscious about the Buddhists or Dalit women's contribution in social movement against system of caste inequality. This approach created impact on the Buddhist community that they prefer to call Buddhist monk rather Buddhist female monk. Disha, drew the attention towards discriminative process in the regards of Buddhists Monk.

> In dhamma, compared to Buddhists men, female Buddhist are much better and this is because of female actively participation in vihars and conducting programmer. I have seen female Bhikuni is less preferable to Buddhist community compare to male Bhikuni which show less respect to Buddhist female which is setback for Buddhist community's concept of equality. It can be overcome just making conscious about their contribution in social movement of emancipation from the caste slavery.

The discriminative process in Buddhist community has inter-related to marriages. It has been said that marriage usually prevents the liberty of women and make her to adjust in the framework of marriage. In this regard, she has to compromise with her wishes and decision often influence under the male dominance. In general sense, the liberalism of Buddhist men has forwarded by women in comparison to other non-Buddhists women. Vibha Gajbhiya, a financial advisor LIC explains how the Buddhist women after marriage limitizes her wishes and compromise at certain level but at the same time reflect comparative account of Buddhist women and non-Buddhist women.

> I have more space compare to other women. But in a very limited manner, I feel marriage is compromise where we have to squeeze our wishes but at the same time we get stronger support from our husband. I tell you Buddhist men are more liberal than other men. I have got lot of opportunity to develop my personality. Limitation mean to me, when I compare men with women in general we find that men never tolerate his wife being more intelligent or smarter than him. Sometime we have to show them that we are not less in capacity and intelligent than anyone including him also. You know when I say Buddhist men is liberal in the relation to Buddhism which I feel they may be understanding women position but unable to control his patriarchic cal mind … he may be understand and one day he will come to follow the concept of equality rooted in our religion.

If the women are not locating in place of equality, would create vacuum in modernistic values of liberty, equality and fraternity. Another respondent claims that those who haven't accept the basic thoughts of Buddha and Ambedkar is still in the clutches of patriarchy and follow its function to dominate women. According to Nandeshwar, she asserted that Buddhist identity could be developed only by negating the patriarchy system. It also mentioned that educated parents can internalize the seeds of equal opportunity to their next generation only by adopting Buddhists thesis.

> Ya we don't have space and I agree with it. It is very less percentage of people who have understood it. The reason is not accepting the Buddhists principles of equality, liberty and fraternity. The male dominance we can observe not only in him but also in other caste and religion and we are yet to reach to the level where men enjoy their liberty. I got the space due to my educated parents and they taught about it and make us to learn Buddhism at our home.

From it, an outer world of non-Buddhist could make a reference that the emancipator project Buddhism is held up between those who are endeavouring to overcome from mental slavery of patriarchy and those who are unable to break boundaries of patriarchy system. At this line of thought, Poonam

Pillawer, a lecturer has projected phenomena of liberal scope for development of women at equal par of men. She provides us some element which makes to think that at extent patriarchy has been diluted in some manner.

> I have full liberty at my home. I use to work outside and my husband takes care of all my domestic work including rearing the children. Even my husband parents don't have any objection for it and in reverse of it I always get encouragement from the side of my Husband.

Caste and Identity Politics

To understand the revolutionary step taken by Dr Ambedkar against caste system and declaration of renouncing Hinduism, one has to take the journey of historical account of parallel religious ideology of Vedic religion and Buddhism. It is agony that exploration of Buddhism in ancient India has been taken from the Hindu's religion's point of view. Thus, the conversion of untouchable community like Mahar into Buddhism is a process of revival of Buddhism which India has lost in the time of ancient India. After the conversion, it was expected that Buddhists as new identity would vanish the caste identity and liberate India from system of social stratification rooted in caste inequality. In other words, the realization came upon may be among the neo-Buddhist that conversion of religion will not bring about their economic and social status of neo-Buddhist and fundamental change in the whole social system is necessary (Singh 2008: 155). There is no doubt that Buddhist community has progressed in every sphere of life where they feel confident and proud to be Buddhists. Thus, it is imperative to explore whether the newly acquired identity is able to replace the stigmatized identity of caste within Buddhist community and in the perception of non-Buddhist. The respondent of Buddhist community has mixed feeling about the caste discrimination within Buddhist community women in relationship with non-Buddhist women. It has been observed that Buddhist women feel secure in the surrounding Buddhist locality and rarely face any caste discrimination, while in non-Buddhist locality; they have external pressure and perception of caste discrimination. It shows that Buddhist community's perception relay numbers of household situated in which areas of Nagpur. Although, there is change in Buddhist community and perceived identity with more proudly but caste identity has congruence with Buddhist identity from the perception of non-Buddhist. It could be observed in the context of inter-caste marriages where it has been viewed that the notion of caste has been kept under the carpet of difference of culture and tradition in between Buddhists and non-Buddhists. In this regards, Neha, pursuing her graduation, explicitly admit that there is confusion whether discrimination is on the basis of caste or behaviour and eating habits.

> It is not easy to speak anything about what they think about us but one thing is very clear that the perception of non-Buddhist has not changed. This I feel when we call them in our any programmes, they won't come nor they eat in our house. I feel that Buddhists identity has not able to replace caste identity in full manner from non-Buddhist perception but I can say it is in process of making of identity. In villages, there is caste but in city I don't find through the naked eyes.

It is conceived notion of Buddhist women that there might be chance that this perception has not changed due to celebration and following both tradition of Hinduism and Buddhism by Buddhist women. Respondents Kajal (housewife and post-graduate in Pali) and Priya (post-graduate in Ambedkar thought, teacher in corporation school), has not faced caste discrimination because of having Buddhist surrounding around them.

> I have not seen that caste identity has wiped out being Buddhist. The reason may be that women follow both traditions of Hindu and Buddhist or because of surnames which we carry. In this way, women are neither Buddhist nor Hindus. I haven't come across any such type of experience of caste discrimination or being Buddhist might they (non-Buddhist) feel but non-Buddhist has not shown openly …. (Kajol)

> I remember that sometime we face discrimination at community level due to caste but I don't have experience of it as I kept my work perfect nor I have come in contact with

> Non-Buddhist community as I hardly get to time to interact with other community people. Sometime I have observed that Buddhist community use to get discriminated only due to reservation .... (Priya)

Hence, it has to notify that identity used to perpetuate in public sphere from two ways that is perception within the community and perception from outside the community. Due to amalgamation of both religious identities, the Buddhist community is unable to achieve the level of respectful identity. As a result of it, the non-Buddhist in public domain or individual interaction remembered this old identity because of the resemblance in Buddhism and Hinduism. Thus, Sneha Nandeshwar, electronic engineer, preparing for Civil Services Exam, openly put unspoken view of upper castes or non-Buddhist people.

> Yes, we are converted people and Buddhism has not become stronger the way Babasaheb Ambedkar was expecting from us ... even from our personality, we hardly reflect our Buddhism and from our behavior or actions, we reflect Hinduism. This is because we feel that we are part of Hinduism and that's why other also perceives us in the same manner and other castes people make you realize that you're from lower caste. If we accept their notion and thought of caste identity, than we cannot progress in our life.

The new technique has obtained to overcome the caste discrimination and pursue the Buddhist identity by making excellence in every sphere so that no one should raise or question them on the basis of their caste identity. For some respondent, caste is not primary factor rather how they are representing themselves in society and in their working places and their confidence would cease to speak about their stigmatized identity. But other studies focus that militant and literary movement cherished the value of inequality and increased consciousness in educated men and women that in spite of their efforts to change in their identity by conversion, there is not much recognition given to their redefined social position (Shastree 1996: 102). The Alpana Meshram, working as architect in her own company (Alpana Enterprises), enforces to wash out the caste identity through intelligence.

> For me, it is very necessary to be competent or become complete women or by placing your views differ than rest of group of members, than I feel there would not be caste first ... thus, it is depend how you present or represent yourself would definitely take the notice by the people. If you have something, the non-Buddhist person would try to know about you. Even if they come to know about your caste, I don't think that they would speak something about caste before you.

It is usually said that inter-caste marriage is solution for caste system. Through it, there would be sharing of culture and tradition between different castes. It is hard to speak about the successfulness of inter-caste marriages because it has been observed that in inter-caste marriage, any one of the individual has to subordinate to other one in order to maintain this sacred thread. It is reflected in Buddhist community that inter-caste marriages often takes between bride from upper caste and bride-groom from lower caste. It is said that the upper castes bride always marry to economic status quo person of lower caste but it hardly happened in reverse order. The other aspect deals with taking the importance of women in the family by the Dalit communities where the marriage merely depended upon caste background of individual which is very significant for it. The study related marriages, many of Dalit community hide their caste background and very few reflect it without hesitation (Paswan 2003: 247). Its means that person having low economic status never become option for upper caste bride. Hence, the pre-conceived notion of caste identity hides at the back of upper castes on the issues of marriage. For the Buddhist community, it is process of crippling the community by brahmanizing him who could become emancipator of lower castes community and social movement. Thus, Prerna Jambulkar (M.Sc Zoology, B.Ed), working as teacher in junior Science College, and Swati More (M.A., B.Ed), has talked about mentality of other community people in relation caste.

> The Hindu people come together with us and share food with us but somewhere they have caste in their mind that we are SC ... the reasons behind that they are not willing to give their girl for marriage to our community boy but love marriage is different thing. I never feel that other caste women would ask willing SC girl for her son marriage. The roti beti process has not happened as said by Dr Ambedkar. The marriage can bring equality but other caste people are not ready for it. The Buddhist community following the sub caste notion while selecting bridegroom or bride is itself a anti Phule Ambedkarism .... (Prerna)

> We have come from Hindu religion therefore, we have caste identity. We use to identify and remembers us that we are converted people of 1956 conversion. Even though we have converted but still we are same in their eyes. I feel no one say anything before us but at the back of mind we feel caste. They follow mental untouchability. They don't take cognizance of our progress and development by saying O!! He/she is Mahar!! Doesn't know anything. The thing of themselves has not changed but it is not our problem, it is their mentality not ours!! .... (Swati)

Despite having Buddhist identity, the Buddhists people are still in domain of inferiority complex due to unawareness about Buddhism. The other issues prevailing in Buddhist community is that Buddhist identity could not percolate at the level of humanism due to inculcation of caste in government official document and find no difference between Hinduism and Buddhism. As a result of it, the Buddhist people hesitate to identify themselves in public sphere and reflect their constitutional identity. The respondent Indu Pillewar, contributory lecturer in college, post-graduate, find contradiction between Buddhist identity and Schedule Caste.

> Even we have taken diksha but in our official document we find caste. I feel that we should write Buddhist rather than caste. I feel pity for it. In general sense, for outside world, we are Buddhist in our community while enquiring in public we become Schedule caste but never say we are Buddhists. There are other Buddhist communities from lower castes except

Mahar who don't reveal their identity in public just like Mahar. As result of it, there is perception that Mahar has not taken the Buddhism at all.

Conclusion

There is assorted feeling profoundly persisting in the perception of Buddhist women in their own religious identity. Buddhist conversion has created separate identity on paper but could not conceptualize it in their practical behaviour and action. The expectation of Ambedkar to create an idealized society based on Buddhist values is yet to achieve, in which some Buddhist women endeavour to rectify deeds within the community by questioning their faith in Buddhism and loyalty towards Ambedkar's thoughts on idealized society. It discerns that Buddhist community perpetuating the politics of identity within arena of patriarchy and festivals by locating the tool to examine identity of Buddhist. The generalized perception has occurred in the context of caste perception of non-Buddhist. Despite, 56 years of development in the field of socio-economic and politics, it is scrutinized that caste of mind doesn't show any transformation towards acquiring new identity as Buddhist. It seems that Mahar caste as an identity has established the same symmetrical phenomena with new identity as Buddhist.

References

Issac Venema, Henery, 2000, *Identifying Selfhood: Imagination, Narratives and Hermeneutics in the Thought of Paul Ricoeur*, SUNY Press, New York.

Jevtic, Miroljub, 2007, 'Political Science and Religion', *Politics and Religion Journal*, Vol. 1, No. 1.

——, 2008, 'Religion and Relations between Genders', *Politics and Religion Journal*, Vol. 2, No. 1.

Mcquillan, Martin, 2000, *The Narrative Reader*, Routledge, London.

Paswan, Sanjay, 2002, *Encyclopedia of Dalits in India: Women*, Vol. 9, Gyan Publishing House, New Delhi.

——, 2003, *Encyclopedia of Dalits in India: Human Rights: New Dimensions in Dalit Problems*, Vol. 14, Gyan Publishing House, New Delhi.

Shastree, Uttara, 1996, *Religious Converts in India: Socio-Political Study of Neo-Buddhist*, Mittal Publications, New Delhi.

Singh, N.K., 2008, *Contemporary Indian Buddhism: Tradition and Transformation*, Global Vision Publishing House, New Delhi.

Tewari, Babita and Sanjay Tewari, 2009, 'The History of Indian Women: Hinduism at Crossroads with Gender', *Politics and Religion Journal*, Vol. 3, No. 1.

Viswanathan, Gauri, 1998, *Outside the Fold: Conversion, Modernity and Belief*, Princeton University Press, Princeton, NJ.

6

Social Dynamics in a Religious Milieu

The Sevayats of the Jagannath Temple at Puri

Ramanuj Ganguly

History of human kind shows us that religion has played a vital role in the formation of civilization and has influenced the course of its events. But in the informed world of today, the influences of industrialization, colonization, world wars, nationalism and social transformation have affected faith and are reshaping our worldview.

Often, social commentators have argued that religious organizations of today are the decadent relics of the past, and then have equated them with a particular religion. But this line of argument tends to get ignored by the society, in general. Religion is normally acquitted of any blame, not reproached for creating any degeneration in a particular religious organization because it is thought to be not capable of doing so. The logic behind such a line of thought is religion and religious organization cannot be equated, as the latter is only a method of religious attainment, therefore is a finite and determinate mediating institution. Further, scholars in today's society find religious organizations to be too narrow and parochial to inform the society about religion that could ensure equity and justice within society, thus found the authority of such moral agency waning. Instead, they stated, that there has been a shift in the location of the moral agencies to the secular institutions and processes of the society, as well as in the thoughts and behaviour of the individual beings. However, going by what we are experiencing in our daily life in India, there is no point in underestimating the importance of religious organizations, rituals, pilgrimage, or festivals in our life. These, I suppose, have to be understood to be human work from which we derive spiritual benefit of being and self, as well as find it to be a moral security net in the times of crisis.

Notwithstanding the rationality and 'affective-neutrality' of contemporary society, it remains inadequate in reinforcing the good will and commitment in human beings that are background conditions for its survival. Religion is still thought to have more value to humans than their other earthly bonds that are mostly forced, transitory and provisional in nature. Therefore, contrary to the expectation of religion being an anathema in the 21st century, it continues to play a fundamental role in the society.

Here, it is not the task to ask whether God exists or not, or the truth of a religious doctrine, rather it aims to provide a sociological analysis of meaning of religious activities in the society and the place of religion in the life of human beings. Therefore, instead of depending on the textual understanding of transcendental static social structures, or universal theories of religion, or analysis of universal cultural norms, effort is to understand the dynamic interrelationship between religious organizations, the agent, and the present society involved in constantly producing codes and representations, thereby, analyse the nature and composition of social life.

To grasp the Indian way of life, the European Colonizers, Western scholars and following them the Indian scholars, with a few exceptions, have drawn simplistic generalizations, neglecting 'multitude of agents involved in the production of culture' (Banerjee Dube 2001: 6). Epistemological assumptions of concepts like caste society, Asiatic Mode of Production or Oriental Despotism that try to explain Indian society are at best partial and mostly distorted. Unilinear evolutionary models of continuum with two polar types have been used for understanding Indian reality but has the difficulty of comparison between entities of different order (Indradeva and Shrirama 1999: 22). Radically opposed models, such as sacred – profane, pure and impure, right and left, readily used for understanding Indian society are at best useful tools in the analysis of particular cases but are not ends in themselves. Temple has always been relegated to a subordinate place in comparison to caste, lineage and village, though it presents 'an alternative locus from which to consider these larger issues' (Appadurai 1981: 8–9). Though temples and sacred places have worked as unifying forces of all – Indian tradition – but the methodological insulation amongst the sociologists, Indologists, historians and social anthropologists have led to a situation where in dichotomically isolated concepts have been juxtaposed to show the cultural developments of India. To fix the nature of Indian culture in particularistic terms exhibit less delicate sensibilities on the part of the researchers towards the distinctive pattern of 'continuous and fluid process of accretion' that has taken place in the growth of Indian culture (Eschmann et al. 1978: xiii).

In face of present day forces of industrialization, urbanization and changing social configuration, personal worship, worship in temple, guidance of spiritual authorities and pilgrimage, continue to inform and shape the values of Indians. A case in point is the Shri Jagannath Temple, at Puri, Odisha, prominent and popular till today, upholds the composite culture of India for more than 900 years.

The present temple complex was constructed after 1135 AD by the Ganga King Anantavarman Chodagangadeva (1078–1147) on the ruins of an earlier temple built by the Kesari King, Yayati Kesgari. Since then, for around nine centuries, in the face of social, economic and political ups and downs, the Sevayats have survived and emerged as the most faithful upholders of this enigmatic religious tradition that is designed as a symbol of universal brotherhood and synthesis of diverse religious trends, besides acting as a message of peace.

It was Anangabhimdeva (1211 AD) who foresaw the need for disciplined administration of the Temple and introduced the system of 'Chattisa Niyoga' (36 types of Sevayat) in the place of original nine types of Sevayat. Niyoga are an association of each category of Sevayat with distinct duties, organized for effective execution of daily rites and rituals within the temple. Proportionate to their ritual functions Sevayats enjoyed part of the 'Amrit Mahoni' (rent free land) and 'Khei' (Kotho Bhog offering).

In the course of time, increasing endowments made to the temple necessitated greater elaboration of ritual services and worship. This led to a subdivision and bifurcation of the various niyogas to independent niyogas. In the Record of Rights (Panda 1955) 119 categories of Sevayats are indicated but the census of the Sevayats conducted by Sri Jagannath Temple Administrative Committee 1988 showed 63 types of Sevayats were present.

The Sevayats of different castes, regardless of their contemporaneous social rank were accorded equal status and importance considering their association and engagement in the temple. Though this did not affect their ethos, the unique method of organization among the Sevayats in the Jagannath Temple reflected a virtual liberalism and imparted a democratic character to the entire organization.

Puri, over a millennium, has been important to the population of this subcontinent due to the location of Sri Jagannath Temple. This paper undertakes to explain the purpose and motivation of the singularly important human element that upholds this religious institution, their current situation and future expectations. This can in the process help us understand the underlying strands of integration that binds Indian society still.

Method

This paper primarily deals with the Sevayats, who are part of a complex religious organization, centring round the Jagannath Temple, at Puri. The Jagannath Temple at Puri remain embedded in the Indian way of life because of two reasons, namely, due to the ritual specialists (here the Sevayats), who by effective execution of daily rites and rituals within the temple have upheld the faith of the masses and held them around the holy symbols, and due to the pilgrim's undying devotion towards the God despite all odds.

Therefore, the endeavour here is a detailed contextual analysis of a limited number of units, their conditions and their relationships. In this investigation the object is to study in depth by using a variety of data gathering methods that is expected to produce evidence leading to understanding of the phenomenon and fulfill the research objectives that targets to unravel a limited number of events, conditions and their inter-relationships.

Data that was collected were qualitative and also quantitative in nature. It was felt that to understand the rationale underlying the relationships in this study could be sufficiently understood only if the collected quantitative data is reexamined in context of qualitative data so that the findings are mutually corroborated and supported. Tools to collect data included direct interviews, observation, and collectio of information from related sources. Due to the unique nature of the field, the investigator had to be flexible in approach in order to accommodate unforeseen changes in interaction pattern, missed appointments by the respondents, or lack of proper environment. The investigator also had to be sensitive about the fact that the respondents despite of their faith and rapport with the investigator may have a niggling un-surety about the purpose of the current study, and of what this study will ultimately bring out for them. Repeat interviews, of focused and brief in nature, with the sampling units were necessary number of times to gather additional information, clarify contrary responses, re-ascertain key observations and sometimes to simply cross-check a claim.

This paper is based on the study where the population comprised of all the Sevayats of Jagannath Temple, whose total population size was 3,802 (Temple Census 1988). All the units were male and hereditarily attached to the temple, with specific seva (ritual functions). There are 63 categories of Seva or Sevayats presently performing ritual functions within the temple. For this study, out of these 63 categories of Sevayats, 18 categories are the primary sampling units which were randomly selected, constituting more than 28 per cent of the total representative population. Further, from these 18 categories, 5 per cent of the units were randomly selected from each category as the secondary sampling unit, based on the temple Census, 1988. Thus we reached the sample size of 145. The reasons why such a method of sample selection was adopted were the constraints of data availability as well as the nature of the study, which does not want to singularly restrict itself only to quantitative analysis of data. The method of data collection from each sampling unit was done with help of an interview schedule that included both close-ended and open-ended questions. The mediating factors for successful administration of the interview schedule were also possible because of the personal background of the investigator. For better insight, a whole lot of other people involved with the temple in some way or other, be it in the administration or related businesses or informed private individuals, were discussed with. Also, the investigator was able to gather a lot of information by non-participant observation of the Sevayats' activities, and by listening to the discussions that the Sevayats have in their leisure period within the temple complex. So while analysing, all these information were used to enrich and interpret the data collected through the interview schedule.

It is expected that we will understand not only the changing nature of the differences in the social status among the Sevayats in present times, but also examine the attitude of the Sevayats towards the changes that are taking place in the greater society in the present times, and their perception about the consequent factors that are affecting their life. Though importance of caste in the social lives of the Sevayats and the nature of interrelationship among the niyogas and Sevayats within the temple are issues that have a determined effect on their lives but it is far more important to consider whether there has been any change in the strength of the religious faith and conviction among the Sevayats, over the years. To gain an insight about the future condition of their community, here we will try to see whether the attraction of the younger generation of the Sevayats towards their hereditary ritual occupation in the temple has changed and if so, the factors behind their changing perception. Related to this, we need to examine whether the minimum economic security provided by the hereditary ritual occupation in the temple works as a de-motivating factor for the younger generations to seek alternative secular occupation. Keeping the changes in last six decades in India, we do need to see whether religious consideration play a role in the political participation of the Sevayats, and has there been any change in the economic condition of the Sevayats presently, in comparison to the past.

Socio-Economic Background of the Sevayats

For analysis of the data, the sampled Sevayats were categorized into three categories, according to their ritual function within the temple, which are as following:

- Category A, 62 in numbers comprising of Sevayats who perform ritual function within sanctum sanctorum.
- Category B, 68 in numbers comprising of Sevayats who perform ritual function outside the sanctum sanctorum.
- Category C, 15 in numbers comprising of non-brahmin Sevayats and those who trace tribal lineage.

The mean age of the sample is 50 years, and the distribution of the sample in three age groups – Young (15–35 years) covering 24.14 per cent, Middle (35–55 years) covering 34.48 per cent, Old (55 and above years) covering 41.38 per cent.

In terms of education the Sevayat community is yet to achieve the level that could give them capacity to bring a substantial change in their quality of life. Though mean effective years of education of Sevayats are just 07.64 years, but if compared to age and their children's education then we see that there is a very distinct intergenerational transformation taking place among them. There is an inverse relation between age and education, which means that among Sevayats, in last 50 years more and more people have gone for secular education. Significantly, among respondents below the age of 35 years, there is no illiteracy, and those who have children, all are into education. Illiteracy is acute among the aged, and it seems illiteracy breeds' illiteracy. When education and niyogas are compared, we see that illiteracy is most acute among the third category of Sevayats, i.e. the non-Brahmin Sevayats. Less than one-fourth Sevayats in category A and just more than that in category B, whereas more than half of category C are illiterates.

Among the respondents who have married and have adult children show that the next generation is better qualified than their parent's generation irrespective of gender. But it was observed that Sevayats still do not recognize that women need to go for much higher education because they do not foresee their daughter to have much activity beyond their home. Further, education still does not count much in the 'marriage-market' for the sevayat community which can be seen as a reason for their girl children not pursuing higher education to the extent in comparison with their male counterpart in the family.

For the Sevayats of Sri Jagannath Temple it was seen that Niyoga identity is unique and provide them a status level in the greater society that is better than Jati identity. They take advantage of the society's ignorance about the presence of non-Brahmin Sevayats in the temple. Further, as Sevayats they are accorded equal status among themselves, therefore, in terms of their interrelationship they find niyoga as more suitable for their activities. As far as marriage and taking up of secular occupation are concerned Sevayats do give importance to caste consideration as well as to their status as Sevayats. In case of matrimonial alliances they prioritize partnership from sevayat community, otherwise among *Jatis* that are considered of equal or higher plain. They were firm that because of their Jati consideration and especially their hereditary occupation in the Temple, notwithstanding an individuals academic or technical qualification or economic compulsion, if somebody goes singularly for secular occupation outside the temple, they should refrain from taking up 'menial jobs' as they are considered incompatible to their Jati and Niyoga status. It is interesting to note that a Sevayat youth will readily accept a job of a peon in a government office yet would not accept a management trainee in a hotel because he has to perform jobs in the laundry section or in the kitchen/restaurant. The social pressure on the family is also enormous which forces them to not to take up such occupation. It can be inferred that Jati and Niyoga membership as a whole, irrespective of all the independent variables, is an impediment for the Sevayat community to take up secular occupations compatible to their level of qualification and skill. In case of accepting *daan* or gifts from pilgrim patrons they do not discriminate on these lines.

Another interesting finding in this regard, is the fact that Jati or niyoga membership in no way affects their political decision-making process. As a group Sevayats of Jagannath Temple can swing a party's fortune in elections of Puri town. From Puri, known for its religious heritage, never a political party with religious ideals or affiliations has ever won an election. In fact, they were found to be skeptical in their attitude towards political parties with religious ideals or affiliations. Also they are very conscious in dealing with their *Jajman* because in no way they are ready to jeopardize their prospect of earning.

Monthly income as stated by the Sevayats shows that, in today's standards Sevayats have pretty low income. Around 43 per cent of Sevayats earn between ₹ 0–4000 per month, and around same percentage earn between ₹ 4000–8000 per month. But here a few considerations, as observed, have to be factored in for better understanding of the situation. First, Sevayats are in habit to exhibit exaggerated accounts of their misery to the pilgrims. Second, their humble lifestyle and unscheduled dispersed income style many times do not allow them to even realize their actual income. Third, a lot of perquisite that comes with the job is taken for granted by the Sevayats and are not included by them in their income. Fourth, while calculating income in terms of the standards of today's world, even then, it has been observed that Sevayats as a whole belong to low-income category. When income was understood in relation to education, niyoga and family size, it was seen that formal education does not have a very significant impact on the income of the Sevayats. In most of the niyogas as well as between the niyogas income distribution is uneven and polarized. In comparison to the family size, per head income distribution is pretty low. Income, therefore, has to be understood in terms of the importance of the ritual function within the temple, and from sources that are external to the temple though it may directly or indirectly be related to the temple. Importance of the ritual function within the temple generates better revenue from the pilgrim patrons or creates condition that results in better probability of getting a pilgrim patron. Hospitality business, sale of Mahaprasad, and local craft and textile are various other avenues that the Sevayats exploit for their own income.

Majority of the Sevayats (75.17%) agree that their income has gone up. The reasons shown for rise in the income are: (a) more pilgrim visitors; (b) people's contribution has gone up; (c) better communication facility; (d) increase in the fame of the temple; (e) *puraskar* from the temple administration; (f) improved employment and business opportunities. Though most of the Sevayats consider their income to have gone up, yet they are conscious of the fact that in real term it has gone down. Reasons shown for their feeling that rise in income has not been real so as to affect their lives are: (a) division of jajmans amongst brothers; (b) increase in number of dependents; (c) areligious attitude of people; (d) rise in the population of the Sevayats; (e) outsiders working in the temple; (f) vestment by the State Government of landed property held by the Sevayats; (g) value of money has gone down due to inflation.

Further, as because they distinguish between what they earn and the value of their earning in terms of market prices, we can say that Sevayats are getting influenced by the consumerist trends and necessities, evident from the fact that use of modern amenities and accessories by the sevayat families.

Group Interrelationship: Dynamics

The Sevayats are of the view that though ideally they supposedly should enjoy equal status and importance, but in reality among them there is wide level of difference in every aspect of their activity. They feel that it is the economic considerations and consequent power that it generates which creates the differences. The rich and the powerful Sevayats are in a position to manipulate the niyogas' decisions in their favour. Thus, they take a leadership position within the niyoga. Pilgrims, who are outsiders, also get influenced by the economic might and resources of these Sevayats who are able to cater better service to them. Better position within the niyoga and patronage from the pilgrims naturally provide these few Sevayats with higher economic returns. The administration with their motive to singularly ensure timely performance of rites and ritual keep these Sevayats in good humour so that through them they can control the Sevayat community better in their duties. Also they know that the powerful Sevayats have more nuisance value and can create trouble within the temple.

Sevayats agree that these factors do not work in isolation rather are complementary in nature creating differences within the Sevayat community. Most of the Sevayats were of the view when asked about the interrelationship among themselves, that compared to past, the relationship among Sevayats has taken a turn for worse; the past was better because the relationship was more intimate, free, frank, and did not trample anybody's credulity. At present the relationship stands more on mistrust, selfish motivation and hegemony. Apparent bonhomie and organized conflict is the real state of relationship among Sevayats. On a general plain the Sevayats agree that they are a divided lot because of differential ritual importance within the temple, uneven economic income, uneven official patronage, and limited opportunity and resources that ultimately results in subordination – superordination between the niyogas.

The issue of differential importance given/attached to the various ritual functions assigned to particular niyogas is though thought to be a major reason for difference in influence and power between the niyogas. But it seems the Sevayats are divided on the issue. Though more than half of them consider it is the ritual function that they perform within the temple as the cause of difference but almost the other half of the respondents feel that it is factors like income, number of jajmans, combined with the nature of ritual function that affects the cause.

Despite all the difference between them the Sevayats also unite in times of self-interest or exigencies. Image of the temple being their only capital for survival, Sevayats always want to keep the pilgrims in good humour. Contradiction towards this end creeps in because they also want to extract maximum revenue from the pilgrims. Mass participation as witnessed in the temple gives ample opportunity for unhealthy practices, but Sevayats on their own do ensure the security of the pilgrims.

The niyogas are vigilant about the activities of the administration, and they contest all one-sided actions. They are mostly conscious of the fact that if the administration is given a free hand, their sphere of influence may get contracted. But mostly the administration does take any action that affects the hegemony of the Sevayats within the temple.

In case of disputes, the secretary and other leaders of the concerned niyoga try and resolve it; otherwise, it is referred to the temple administration who then resolve it. The general impression is that, the solution or justice is mostly unfair, often tilting in favour of the high and mighty. As the administration has to run the show hassle free, expediently it takes side of those who can influence their reach within the temple. Administration also takes advantage of Sevayat's disunity due to which they have a weak bargaining power.

In this section, it becomes evident that the Sevayats are a divided lot, who for short term gains and mutual benefit go along with each other. Economic consideration is the major factor that divides them as well as brings them together. Deep seeded mistrust results in unbridgeable schisms and factionalism that hinders their collective welfare. Taking advantage of this, the outsiders and administration of the Temple can get away with a lot of acts of omission and commission. They realize that it is necessary for them to unite for the betterment of the lot but they cannot bridge the gap because of vested interest. It is observed that the interdependency simultaneously encourages contradictory processes as well as unite them in their daily activities.

Changing Perception: Organization and Profession

The Sevayats are conscious of the fact that the quality of performance of rites and rituals has gone down. They are of the view that age and experience does give a sevayat more efficiency, but mundane considerations like income of the temple, providing maximum access to the pilgrims, political pressure, commercial compulsions many a times forces a sevayat to compromise with the quality. Further, the under trainee Sevayats are bred with inadequate training. Overall we can conclude that the Sevayats agree that ritual performance, compared to past, is of lower quality. Though majority of the Sevayats feel that dedication and sincerity of the younger generation remain unchanged, but when seen in relation to age it was seen that more than 83 per cent of the aged Sevayats feel that dedication and sincerity of the younger generations have gone down. Despite of all the changes that the Sevayats are experiencing as members of the sevayat community as well as a part of the greater society, they feel that the young Sevayats continue to have faith in the institution, irrespective of factors like age, education or income. This is one major reason why continuity of the temple and ritual performance within it continues without much hassle.

Irrespective of age, income, education and niyoga, the Sevayats mostly want their future generations to continue in their hereditary profession. But they also mentioned that their future generation should also seek supplementary source of income. They feel if not all, at least one son should remain engaged in this profession. They consider that this profession is the result of their good fortune and the good deeds of their past life, secular occupation under no circumstance they can forgo this.

Sevayats those who directly deal with pilgrims are of the view that sevayat-pilgrim interrelationship is apparently cordial and friendly. Yet, the level of confidence in this relationship, according to the Sevayats, seems to have waned. They feel that Sevayats do not portray a sophisticated image that is in consonance with present day sensibilities. Economic compulsions of the Sevayats (mostly the *dhulias*) also force many of them to haggle with the pilgrims for ***dakshina***, which leaves a lasting negative impression about them.

The respondents agreed that the visitors'/pilgrims' religiosity have gone down from past; with changed social environment and changed priorities in life the visitor/pilgrim have very limited interest in rituals (which is where the

Sevayats have a role to play), and are skeptical about the Sevayats, who lack sophistication in articulation, but are high-strung to earn as much as possible, mostly giving a wrong impression about themselves.

Strikingly, every respondent showed that they do not understand the meaning of the word 'role' (here roughly meaning *boomika/abadaan*) nor have the imagination to grasp it. On the contrary, uniformly and generally they have expressed their life situation, which according to them: the position of the Sevayats in today's society is bad, rather despicable.

Religious performance in today's society is as materially motivated as any other enterprise, where depending on the surety and quantum of returns, people engage and spend. Secular occupation except as a means of show-off, people hardly are committed towards ritual performance in light of the above, therefore it is but natural that the Sevayats are merely a necessary evil, a residue, mechanically upholding a highly acclaimed tradition, but are unsure of their standing. It is this neglect that is further cloistering their life.

This hinders their progression and adjustment in tune with the attitude of the society. They brood about their past, regret about the missed opportunities, aware about the rot within the community, yet unable to shrug-off the inertia they are in. Isolated and uncertain they are, but they have to interact daily with the greater society for their own survival as well as to uphold the bestowed hereditary tradition – where in they are looked down upon.

The Sevayats of Jagannath temple at Puri are gradually realizing that secular occupations are more remunerative and socially more acceptable. Education is a significant factor for the younger generations in their realization that only depending on the temple for their survival will not allow them to have a life that is at par with the present day social trends. Yet, they are of the view that because of their slowness in the attitude change, education has not yet made the necessary impact that can raise their overall income or can change their ethos and lifestyle. They accept that education does de-motivate the younger generation towards their hereditary occupation. Those who excel in education, by far very nominal in number, do of course continue pursuing it further and mostly tend to not come back to their hereditary occupation until they retire from these pursuits. At the same time a considerable number of Sevayats feel that low education and high unemployment among the Sevayats results due to the low priority given to any thing that is not connected to the temple. Further, at the back of the mind it is always there that if something does not work out, they always can fall back upon the temple and their hereditary occupation, that at least will ensure subsistence level income. 'No income/work' is not a scenario that a Sevayat can visualize as the temple always attracts pilgrims by its huge and diverse activities. Therefore they mostly tend to see secular occupation complementary to their hereditary occupation.

Though Sevayats from the young age group overwhelmingly disagree, but the middle aged and old Sevayats feel that the economic security provided by the ritual occupation actively works as a deterrent for the youngsters to go for the needful qualification required for competing in the open market for secular occupation. Those who have better education they do not consider that ritual occupation actively works as a deterrent for the youngsters to go for the needful qualification, whereas the Sevayats with less effective years of education tends to agree with this view. The view of the Sevayats on this subject and the nature of their ritual function in the temple are inversely related, i.e. the more important is the nature of ritual function in the temple the more is the disagreement with the view that ritual occupation actively works as a deterrent for the youngsters to go for the needful qualification.

Conclusion

The status, behaviour and values of the Sevayats have undergone a major change in the context of the changed social milieu at the macro level. Changes in the administration had started taking place from the time of British rule and culminated under the government administration in the post-independent India. Under the British rule although the administrative power remained with the King, steps were taken for the proper account of the earnings, and wealth of the temple and its protection. For proper execution, the temple organization was streamlined and reoriented in accordance with the tradition. The British refrained from getting involved in economic liability and performance of rites and rituals. Nevertheless we can conclude that the British rule had brought an element of discipline into the temple organization, which collapsed immediately after the country gained political independence.

It was decisive intervention by the Government that took over temple administration in 1960 that stemmed the rot. Three major changes, took place, which consequently affected the social configuration around the temple. First, clear-cut demarcation among rituals, rites and duties were made. Second, the administration undertook measures to collect financial resources directly from the temple via various means as Hundi. The other sources of earnings (such as property) of the temple were recorded and audited. The government officials in charge were made accountable to the Managing Committee that included the King, the administrator, learned people, and representative of the Sevayats. Thirdly, the effect of land reform measures led to dwindling patronage from the Kings and the landlords. Naturally, the Sevayats were the hardest hit since they were the actual landlords of the Lord's land donated by the Kings, and had enjoyed the part of the proceeds with impunity. The redistribution of the land for actual cultivation or its vestment with the government eliminated this income and the social security thereof. The Sevayats were suddenly left with their only 'secondary' source of income-patronage of the pilgrims. Naturally, the fight and bid for 'dakshina' and donations from the pilgrims became sought after for sheer economic reasons, a trait that is attributed to this group of society. Even today improved transport and communication facilities have altered the composition and character of the visitor in several fundamental ways. Not only has it extended the visitor's market but the quantum of influx for the whole year has also spiralled up. Education, changes in values and religions experiences, changed the priorities and the lifestyle of the visitors. This has in turn drastically affected the profession of the Sevayats and the conditions under which they practice. It is clear that present day society is not only skeptical about the Sevayats, but find their 'sales talk' dubious and 'tasteless'. It is also rather easy to stigmatize them or term them conveniently as losers in the changed social structure, but it would be objective if we try to understand them at the micro level, in context of the changes in social structure at the macro level.

Analytically, we can distinguish between the spiritual complex, where pan-Hindu devotion to Lord Jagannath is pivotal, and the ritual complex, where the Sevayats are its focus, with their specific beliefs and modes of worship. To the visitors, such organizational differences are as immaterial to them as all the ritual acts to acquire merit. Though Brahminical Sanskrit texts positions the Brahmans at the top of the hierarchy, but in reality the Sevayats are perceived to be 'illiterate, ill-behaved, devious, and dangerous'. However, historical changes have affected the value orientations of the Hindus and this explains the contradiction of the Sevayats being tolerated by the visitors, not withstanding their ill repute.

Like every religious centre, amongst the Sevayats of Lord Jagannath Temple, there is a 'front stage' for rituals and belief, and a 'back stage' of conflicts over petty interests. The changes at the macro level have created a completely impersonal pilgrimage market (visitors to the temple for instance are no longer pilgrims, but tourists). A break away from the past has taken place where the jajmani relation between patrons and the Sevayats has been diluted to a great extent. More and more visitors to the temple are unattached or are oblivious of their traditional relations. The economic security provided by such relations is therefore waning. With clear cut demarcation and identity, and accretive group like the Sevayats often try to bring about internal cohesion but always fail to close their ranks. The growing ranks of ' Dhulias' among the Sevayats, who only give ritual service in lieu receive fees is a major development that has taken place during the last 30 years. Another marked trend has been for the few Sevayats, who were able to keep their property to not only try and monopolize on the entire inflow of pilgrims with the help of 'gomastas', but also diversify into other fields of economic activity as opportunities increase. This is a major cause of conflict and jealousy, which clearly shows the mental makeup of the Sevayats. The centrality of financial transactions and the vital role played by middlemen has naturally resulted in the impoverishment of majority of Sevayats and relative success of a few Sevayats.

If we have a close look at the lifestyle of the Sevayats, in the light of the above factors, we find that the majority of the Sevayats are stagnating and failing to utilize the expanding economic opportunities. With a dwindling income and a definite loss of traditional sources of income, the picture of Sevayats haggling to extract money from visitors, has become commonplace in this society. The meagre amount of 'puraskar' and 'Khei' does not relive the Sevayats much. In such a compelling economic situation, the role of government officials in charge of the temple is more opportunistic, who rather than create unnecessary hassles and conflicts with the powerful Sevayats tend to concentrate on the disciplined performance of rites and rituals. Therefore, we should not expect to see any far-reaching changes under government administration, only efforts to maintain the status quo and business as usual.

Generally, though, the religious organization is continuing and its halo is spreading across the world, but the two most important social groups bound to the organization, the Hindu visitor and the Sevayats, seem to live with a perpetual sense of wrongful deprivation. The visitors are harassed and duped continually in the name of religion while the struggle for the Sevayats and their activities are primarily based on survival. What is really required, as in the temple, with its daily rites and rituals, the Sevayats should also be taken care of. It may be practical if a system of registration of all visitors is introduced and the whole sequence of 'Puja-dakshina-prasad' becomes scheduled. This would ensure that the visitors do not get duped and every Sevayat would be given an equal opportunity. This may seem revolutionary but in the last 900 years, the Lord, the temple and the Sevayats have witnessed a lot of catastrophes, inventions and epochal changes. They have survived and have remained open to the developments in society.

References

Appadurai, Arjun, 1981, *Worship and Conflict under Colonial Rule: A South Indian Case*, CUP, Cambridge.

Banerjee Dube, Ishita, 2001, *Divine Affairs: Religion, Pilgrimage and the State in Colonial and Postcolonial India*, IIAS, Shimla.

Copley, Antony, 1997, *Religions in Conflict: Ideology, Cultural Contact and Conversion in Late-Colonial India*, OUP, Delhi.

Das, Nilakantha, 1958, *Orissa Historical Research Journal*, Vol. VII, No. I.

Dube, S.C., 1974, *Contemporary India and its Modernization*, Vikas Publishing House, Delhi.

Eschmann, A., H. Kulke and G.C. Tripathi, 1978, *The Cult of Jagannath and the Regional Tradition of Orissa*, Manohar, New Delhi.

Fuller, C.J., 1984, *Servants of the Goddess*, CUP, Cambridge.

——, 2004, *Hindu Worship, Collected in India's Religion*, edited by T.N. Madan, OUP, New Delhi.

——, 2006, *Renewal of the Priesthood: Modernity and Traditionalism in South Indian Temple*, OUP, New Delhi.

Hamel, J., S. Dufour and D. Fortin, 1993, *Case Study Methods*, Sage, Newbury Park, CA.

Indradeva and Shrirama, 1999, *Society and Culture in India*, Rawat Publications, Jaipur.

Jevtic, Miroljub, 2007, 'Political Science and Religion', *Politics and Religion Journal*, Vol. 1, No. 1.

——, 2008, 'Religion and Relations between Genders', *Politics and Religion Journal*, Vol. 2, No. 1.

Kar, Shashadhar (ed.), 2000, *Puri Guide*, Nilachal Publications, Puri.

Mahapatra, K.N., 1954, *Orissa Historical Research Journal*, Vol. III, No. 2.

Marglin, F.A., 1984, *Wives of God King: The Rituals of the Devdasis of Puri*, OUP, Delhi.

Miles, M.B. and A.M. Huberman, 1984, *Qualitative Data Analysis: A Sourcebook of New Methods*, Sage, Beverly Hills, CA.

Mishra, K.C., 1971, *The Cult of Jagannath*, Firma KLM, Calcutta.

Mohapatra, Gopabandhu, 1981, *God in Three Images at Puri*, Dharma Jyoti Pitha, Puri.

Mol, Johannis J., 1978, 'Introduction', in Johannis J. Mol (ed.), *Identity and Religion: International and Cross-Cultural Approaches*, Sage, London.

Nayak, G.C., 1999, 'The Unique Vedantic Synthesis in Jagannath as Lokayata Bramha and Vaishnavism: A Philosophical Approach', *The Quarterly Journal of the Mythic Society*, Bangalore, July–September.

Patnaik, Himanshu S., 1994, *Lord Jagannath: His Temple, Cult and Festivals*, Aryan, New Delhi.

Pattanaik, Nityananda, 1977, *Cultural Tradition in Puri*, IIAS, Shimla.

——, 2000, *Sacred Complex in Orissa*, Gyan Publishing House, Delhi.

Saraswati, Baidyanath, 1984, *The Spectrum of the Sacred: Essays on Religious Tradition of India*, Concept, New Delhi.

Shah, A.M., B.S. Baviskar and E.A. Ramaswamy (eds), 1998, *Social Structure and Change: Religion and Kinship*, Vol. 5, Sage, New Delhi.

Sri Jagannath Mandir Sevayatankar Samajik O Arthanaitik Sarbekshan O Janaganana (Census), 1988, Sri Jagannath Temple Administrative Committee, Puri.

Srinivas, M.N., 1952, *Religion and Society among the Coorgs of South India*, Clarendon Press, Oxford.

——, 1954, 'A Brief Note on Ayyappa: The South Indian Deity', in *Collected Essays*, OUP, New Delhi.

——, 2002, 'The Social Significance of Religion in India', in *Collected Essays*, OUP, New Delhi.

Starza, O.M., 1997, *The Jagannath Temple at Puri: Its Architecture, Art and Cult*, E.J. Brill, Leiden.

Veer, Peter van der, 1988, *Gods on Earth: Religious Experience and Identity in Ayodhya*, OUP, Oxford.

Vidyarthi, L.P., 1961, *Sacred Complex in Hindu Gaya*, APH, Bombay.

7

Sacred Rivers

Energy Resources and People's Power

Susan Visvanathan

The question of water and land have become the politically most sensitive questions today. Rivers are recognized to be ancient embodiments of the gods as well as sites of civilization. The last hundred years have transformed the way we think about rivers and embankments. In Kerala, the Mulla Periyar, with its source in the border of Kerala and Tamil Nadu, which was once called Madras Presidency, faced many public battles regarding not just the use of the water, but the age and viability of the dam. The Malayalis have seen apocalypse in the eroding dam and have led processions and marches till they received assurance that the 19th century Mulla Periyar would be repaired, and a new dam built further downstream by their own state government. Anand Pandian writes of a colonial engineer called Major John Pennycuick who built the dam, and to whom a Tamil ode has been written, extolling his virtues in changing the drylands of Madurai into a silken quilt of green, where women, who were previously used to famines, now bedeck themselves and dance like peacocks and swans. Major Pennycuick who invested his own money in the building of the dam, and requisitioned finances from local people is also thought to have thrown his second wife, pregnant with child into a crack, to seal the dam. There is a famous tantric tradition of human sacrifice to stabilize the new building, which the colonist seems to be implicated in, by which he becomes the cultic embodiment of the artificially created fertility of a once dry area. Is this to say that no sacrifice is sufficient when it comes to the building of dams? Pandian writes, 'The severe famine of 1876–78 temporarily suspended any administrative attention to the project, but the Famine Commission constituted in its wake specifically recommended the plan to help secure grain production in the hard-hit plains of Madurai. Major John Pennycuick was ordered to assume full responsibility to the proposed project in 1882, and in the same year he submitted a detailed plan that was ultimately sanctioned. The plan called for a thick rubble masonry dam that would eventually rise 176 feet above the riverbed to impound its waters in a large reservoir – water held here would be led through a tributary streambed to a mile-long tunnel blasted through the granite mass of the Western ghats, emerging east to tumble down to the plains of Madura. An agreement was signed with the Government of Travancore to lease the necessary lands in 1886, and work on the dam commenced in 1887. The first waters passed out of the tunnel in 1895' (Pandian 1993 in Baviskar 2003: 14) Interestingly, this is very close to the time the Vice-Regal Lodge in Shimla was electrified after much debate, since the question of coal and gas was being discussed and electricity was seen to be an urgent substitute (Visvanathan 2006). Anand Pandian uses A.T. Mackenzie's *History of the Periyar Project* (1899) to describe the making of the dam. There were tropical forests, wild animals and leeches, half the year was monsoon, and malaria and cholera killed off thousands of workers who found working at 3000 feet tiring enough. 'Hundreds of these labourers perished due to accidents, contagious diseases and climatic exposure – camp hospital registers tell only part of this story as many sick workers went back to their native villages never to appear again at the construction site' (ibid.: 14–15). Pandian comments that the British commemorated their own dead with grave stones, but the Indian workers graveyard remains unmarked and overgrown with scrub. Ecologically, it is significant that many lower caste communities buried their dead in the land allowing for the earth to rejuvenate. British ideas of sedenteriazation of agriculture in Chingleput have been well discussed by Eugene Irschick in *Dialogue and History* (1994) where he suggests for Chingelput that a rural population was created in order to put in place the idea of village society for taxation purposes in the 18th century, where the temple festivals were supported in order to make way for a co-operative and mutually supportive village society (Irschick 1994: 79). Dams would have a similar place in Modern India, except that, displacement would be the key symbol of re-organization of society for the creation of the modern metropolis as the hub of political decision-making, where a pampered middle class would be led to believe that they were the beneficiaries of the policies of the Nation state, and the rest of the population silent witnesses to transformation.

In 1964, Yashoda, the family maid servant, told me that they buried dead ancestors in the yam gardens, and I thought, then, from a eight year old's perspective that was great proximity indeed. My father's brother's wife laughingly said that our jackfruit tree produced such excellent fruit because it was fed from the water of not just the Pamba which flowed by our field, but by the trapped rain water that passed the adjacent graveyard, which had been land gifted from my grandfather's property to the church. This contiguity to river and water is what makes farmers families so alert to the warp and weft of life and death, to subsistence and continuity which are such essential tropes in green movements. India has never stated the problem ideologically as 'agriculture vs industrialization' till very recently, for Gandhi's influence in Nehruvian real politic is very well known. Secularism had its own enchanted spaces. Nehru's fascination for Buddha and Advaitism in the same breath is worthy of analyses. Diana Eck quotes Nehru,

> My desire to have a handful of ashes thrown into the Ganga at Allahabad has no religious significance, so far as I am concerned. I have no religious sentiment in the matter. I have been attached to the Ganga and the Jumna rivers in Allahabad ever since my childhood and, as I have grown older, the attachment has also grown. I have watched their varying moods as the seasons changed, and have often thought of the history and myth and tradition and song and story that have become attached to them through the long ages and become part of their flowing waters. The Ganga, especially, is the river

> of India, beloved of her people, round which are intertwined her racial memories, her hopes and fears, her songs of triumph, her victories and her defeats. She has been a symbol of India's age-long culture and civilisation, ever-changing, ever-flowing, and yet ever the same Ganga. She reminds me of the snow covered peaks and the deep valleys of the Himalayas, which I have loved so much, and of the rich and vast plains below, where my life and work have been cast.' (Eck 2003 in Baviskar 1993: 30, 31)

One of the most brilliant depictions of the Ganges is the work of Michael Aschauer, the Austrian photographer, who had done river length, slow motion studies, of the Danube, the Nile, and went on to photograph the sacred river in Benaras, using a stably placed camera on the roof of a boat as it travelled, along the rim of the holy city.

In Benaras, the questions raised about river pollution have been steadfast. Sacred concerns and scientific ones are mutually supportive, and the activists and the human rights petitioners have used shared resources to fight their battle. The question of Narmada too has always been read as a political and spiritual battle: there has been no conflict in understanding the support that believers receive from secular intellectuals (Baviskar 1993). Amita Baviskar in *In the Belly of the River* (1995) has posed very significant problems of Nation State bias towards industrialization, and the productivity of tribals and peasants vis-à-vis the assumption that poverty rules, by using agricultural statistics and markers of grain production and self-reliance. This data is then juxtaposed with the substitution of the Red Revolutions of the 1950s to 1970s, by the Green Movements in the 1990s, as a symbol of middle class activist preoccupation with the survival of tribal and peasant communities. Milind Ghatwai on the other hand writes that protest movements delay the projects and quotes M.N. Buch. 'He (Buch) says the 'jholawala brigade' opposes everything from nuclear to hydel to thermal power projects.' (Buch also says that) 'Those who benefit should be made to share the spoils with those who are displaced or deprived of their livelihoods, but projects must go on.' Ghatwai also writes, 'What started as a struggle against the Sardar Sarovar Project in the 1980s now encompasses every dam on the Narmada in Madhya Pradesh' (Ghatwai 2012: 9). Speaking on behalf of People's right of life and work, on the other hand are Suvrat Raju and M.V. Ramana,

> Contempt for democracy is as old as democracy itself. The British liberal, John Locke, wrote in 1695 that for 'day-labourers and tradesmen, the spinsters and dairy maids ... hearing plain commands, is the sure and only course to bring them to obedience and practice. The greatest part cannot know, and therefore they must believe.' The Indian ruling classes have evidently taken these medieval ideas to heart. They are simply unable to acknowledge anywhere in India, that farmers and working class people may have a valid and independent perspective on infrastructural projects that must be respected.' (Raju and Ramana 2012: 10)

Ideologically, the plank of development as an industrial representation of so called 'dead villages' being replaced by the metaphors of spatial re-organization is well captured by the book *Village Matters* (Mattison). Here several authors show that traditional systems of irrigation or the preoccupation with small dams is the right of the peasantry, insomuch as these have been creative spaces where they are able to live their lives in harmony with nature. David Harvey, the Marxist geographer who sees the relationship to Nature as a problematic of theory as ideology writes 'I've spent a lot of time trying to persuade engineers that they should take the idea that knowledge, including their own technical ingenuity, is still socially constructed. But when I argue with people from the humanities, I find myself having to point out to them that when a sewage system doesn't work, you don't ring up the postmodernists, you call in the engineers – as it happens, my department has been incredibly creative in sewage disposal' (Harvey 2001: 18).

The petition, accompanying the protest, the inscribed voice of the human rights activist, has been one of the most important ways in which the battle over the future of India with regard to waterways has been fought. Along with this are people's meetings, confrontation with Banks, including the World Bank, and representatives of the Nation state. The use of internet technology and the impact of personalized or collecti web dissemination through the Blog has been considerable. Clearly, the penultimate forum is the Court, and the belief that petitions can be formalized and submitted to the judges for coming to a resolution.

The Ganga has always been a site of myth and riverine subcultures, it's reach so phenomenal, that even it's tributaries are considered sacrosanct. Diana Eck wrote compellingly about the myths of the Ganga, showing that these myths evolve because of love and attention that people give to the river, and that nature worship integrates the indigenous yaksha and naga tradition.

> It is a view in which the universe, and by extension the land of India, is alive with interconnections and meanings and is likened to a living organism. There is no nature 'worship' here, but a sacramental natural ontology. In an excellent essay, Betty Heimann writes: 'In India the veneration of Nature has never been discarded as outdated and primitive. On the contrary, primitivity is here appreciated in its productive ambiguity with inexhaustible potentialities. Nature cult is the fundament of the earliest form of Indian religions and remains the basis of even the highest and most exalted speculations of Indian philosophy.' (Eck 2003 in Baviskar 2003: 33)

However the enthusiasm with which pilgrims throw plastic into the river, or factories their effluents is perhaps the greatest detriment to river cleaning efforts. In their report, Emerging Contaminants in Ganga River Basin with Special Emphasis on Pesticides, Babu et al. argue that,

> The active ingredients in a number of PCPs (personal care products) are considered bioactive chemicals. This implies that they have the potential to affect the flora and fauna of soil and aquatic receiving environments. In some cases, bioactive ingredients are first subject to metabolism by the consumer and the excreted metabolites and parent components are then subject to further transformation in the receiving environment. Personal care products differ from pharmaceuticals in that large quantities can be directly introduced into receiving environments (air, surface and ground water, sewage, sludge

> and bio-solids, landfills, soils) through regular use, such as showering, bathing, spraying, excretion or disposal of expired or used products. Because of this uncontrolled release, they can bypass possible treatment systems. As a result, PCPs are referred to as pseudo-persistent contaminants. (Barceló and Petrovic 2007 in Babu et al. 2001: 3)

The authors also detect steroids in the municipal wastewaters and livestock farming and streams which flow into the river. On a visit to Mathura in 1994, my daughters and I were astounded to see the filth that flew through the streets into the sacred river. Two pundits accompanied us, and one of them jumped into the boat that we took, and then casually took water for us to drink with a cupped palm, exhorting us to drink it, filled though it was with ash and sludge. It turned out he was one of the petitioners in a court case demanding the cleaning of the river in Mathura. All over India, there are people who petition the court to hear their case over the most dramatic of cases, and the spirituality of these places is never denied, though the law is secular. Bharat Jhunjunwala, a former Professor at the Indian Institute of Management, was attacked early this year for petitioning against damming the Ganges, and his activist colleague Vimalbhai, has started a website. In Kerala, sand river mining has become so acute, that the rivers are drying up, and the reclaimed land is silting up rapidly with foliage and trees, so that people used to bathing and worshipping at the sarpu kavus or snake groves, now find that they are literally without a river in the summer months. That rivers have holy value is a visible aspect of our geo-morphology. People of all religions accept this quality, and infact their own stories of origin are related to the sacred river. The St Thomas Christians of Kerala have many stories of floods, floating crosses, and establishment of churches and Christian hamlets wherever such holy emblems were found, as in the case of Niranam where St Thomas is supposed to have made his first Brahman convert. Farming communities have a long history of living in contiguity with each other regardless of their religious differences. Kalpathy River, a sacred river to the Hindus in Kerala, and a tributary of the Neelam and Bharatapuzha, has an annual festival where Muslim and Christian traders have been setting up shops for several centuries according to tradition. Sacred rivers are not only physical manifestations of the divine spirit cleansing people of all castes and religions, for the flowing water does not carry the weight of distinctions, but it also reproduces on its embankments the architecture of it's mythic representation. So, Kalpathy temple in Pallakad Kerala, recreates the steps of Benaras, because the origin of the temple is from the 14th century when it is believed, a Brahman widow walked to Kashi with her husband's ashes and brought back a stone lingam from there, and received the King's patronage in the establishment of a temple at the site where she placed the lingam. Kalpathy, which is now called a Heritage Village, (with laws regarding repair and renovation of it's streets and houses) is a settlement of Smartha Brahmans who lived by their traditional occupations of Astrology, Ayurveda, Accounting, Temple Management, Music and Mathematics, Vedas and its dissemination and of course a very rich food culture. They were not tillers of the soil, so when the land distribution occurred in Kerala, in the 1950s, they lost much of their wealth and property, and since they had been the backbone of the colonial clerical and bureaucratic structures in the Presidency towns, they were able to enter the professional enclaves of modern India very early. One of the fearsome aspects of the river is that since it dries in summer when the Mallapuram dam is shut, and water released for farmers every three days, sand mining is frequently seen as not just predatory but criminal by the local residents who are afraid to speak out, as threats of murder then follow (see Visvanathan 2012).

The Case of Tehri Dam

For the farmer, however, the sacred river stands for agricultural prosperity. An activist has summarized the Neeri Report of 2005 to say that, The Tehri dam 'is also likely to capture around 65 per cent of the total sediment carried by Ganga at present'. In his summary, the Report is thought to valourize the quality of the water for a specific utilitarian purpose, without taking into account how the destruction of algae and phage. I now provide the summary of the Neeri Report sent to me on request, by Dr Bharat Junjhunwala.

- Twenty sampling points were identified in the stretches from Gomukh to Rishikesh and from Badrinath to Devprayag. Maximum five sets of samples were collected from identified sampling points of the rivers (Bhagirathi, Bhilangana, Alaknanda, Mandakini, and Ganga) during September 2002 to August 2003 for assessment of different abiotic, biotic and microbiological parameters.
- Application of water quality index (WQI), which is based on nine parameters, viz. DO, pH, BOD, temperature, total solids, turbidity, total-P, NO_3 and faecal coliform, at various stretches of the river water revealed that water quality of the river between Tapovan and downstream of Uttarkashi was good (index value 70–90) throughout the period of study, while water samples of other areas were ranging medium and good during the same period. An exercise further revealed that WQI values would have been excellent (90–100) throughout the study area, if faecal coliform values were eliminated from the nine parameters used for WQI calculations.
- Based on the irrigation water quality classification, water quality of all the sites of the entire stretch was determined and found to fall under the desired category of C_1S_1. The irrigation quality of water having C_1S_1 category is beneficial for growing plants like: Eucalyptus robusta, Acacia nilotica, Casuarina sp., Prosopis tuliflora, Dalbergia sissoo, Azadirachta indica, etc.
- It has been observed that water samples from different rivers contained specific types of phages. Different types of hosts were required for their detection. The experimentation done at NEERI revealed that Ganga/Bhagirathi sediment has the capability to adsorb coliphages and induce their proliferation. The coliphages adsorbed to the sediment appear to be responsible for predating coliforms in the overlying water column when the sediment and water co-exist in a container under static condition. The Bhagirathi water to be stored in a dam mimics such static condition and, therefore, shall in no way deteriorate the water quality of the river downstream of the Tehri dam.
- The release of copper and chromium under static condition and the synergistic effect of chromium on the

bacteriostatic/bacteriocidal property of copper appear to be the factors which keep the water free from coliforms and other bacteria responsible for putrification of water when left for a long time under static condition.

- Quantification of U_3O_8, ThO_2 and per cent K in sediment samples and comparison of these parameters with those present in other river sediment samples and freshwater lake sediment samples show that Bhagirathi/Ganga sediments collected between Gomukh and Rishikesh are more radioactive than others though it could not be established as to whether the radioactivity observed could be bacteriocidal. However, possibility of existence of synergestic effect of radioactivity on the antibacteriocidal activity of Cu and Cr, in combination, cannot be ruled out.
- It can be concluded now that the uniqueness of river Bhagirathi/Ganga lies in its sediment content which is more radioactive compared to other river and lakewater sediments, can release Cu and Cr which have bactericidal properties and can harbour and cause proliferation (under static condition) of coliphages that reduce and ultimately eliminate coliforms from the overlying water column. This is possible as the dam is going to retain practically all the sediment load of Bhagirathi as particles of size of >0.01 mm are likely to be retained in the dam. Thus, Tehri dam is not likely to affect the quality or self-preservation property of river Bhagirathi/Ganga, as it mimics a static container which is conducive for conditions responsible to maintain the water quality. The NEERI study has honed in on coliphage as the source of the self-purifying capacity of River Ganga. There are two types of bacteria in the river water – coliform are harmful bacteria while coliphage destroy the coliform and are beneficial bacteria. Usually a particular species of coliphage destroys one particular species of coliform. There are innumerable species of both coliphage and coliform. Speciality of Ganga lies in the fact that the coliphage are 'wide-spectrum' – one coliphage destroys many species of coliform.[1] This helps to keep the river's self-purify itself more easily.

Bharat Jhunjhunwala's comment on the NEERI report is useful:

The coliphage are absorbed in the sediments after having been created. They lie dormant in the sediments – even for many years – and get revived when coliform enter the water. NEERI has found that coliphage are present in the river water downstream of Tehri Dam up to Rishikesh. Moreover, NEERI has assessed that 10 per cent release of sediments from Tehri Dam, plus sediments being added by Alaknanda River at Dev Prayag, will be sufficient to supply the sediments required for the coliphage to survive and multiply hence there is no negative impact of Tehri Dam on the self-purifying capacity of the Ganga.

The special quality of Ganga waters is also due to minute (but high) levels of Thorium, which is radioactive, and high levels of copper and chromium in its waters:

It can be concluded now that the uniqueness of River Bhagirathi/Ganga lies in its sediments content which is comparatively more radioactive compared to other rivers and lake water sediments investigated, and can release Cu and Cr which have bactericidal property and can harbour and cause proliferation (under static condition) of coliphages which reduce and ultimately eliminate coliforms from the overlying water column (NEERI 2004: 107).

These beneficial elements – Thorium, Copper and Chromium – enter the river water from the rocks against which the water rubs during flow:

The metal ions, originally derived from breaking of rocks, are controlled by several river valley conditions – physical as well as chemical (NEERI 2004: 74; NEERI 2011: iii).

This absorption takes place in two ways – chemical and mechanical weathering. Rainwater contains miniscule amounts of acid. This acid breaks the rocks and loosens the metals therein which then flow into the river. This is called chemical weathering. Secondly, metals are directly absorbed in the river water as the water dashes against the rocks containing these metals. The difference in metal composition of the river is said to be due to this difference in the weathering regime:

> The striking feature of the radium isotope data is the distinct difference in the 228Ra and 226Ra abundances between the highland and lowland rivers. The lowland waters are enriched in 228Ra, while the highland waters contain more 226Ra. This difference mainly results from the differences in their weathering regimes (NEERI 2011: 169).
>
> The problem is that if upstream river is diverted into tunnels for generation of hydropower then the water will not rub against the stones and not absorb the beneficent metals. It is to be noted that bumper-to-bumper dams have already been made upstream of Tehri Dam except the uppermost 135 km; and are planned on the entire 300 km flow of Alaknanda except the lowest 30 km stretch. Thus it is likely that the coliphages will be deprived of the sediments on which they survive. The metals loosened by chemical weathering due to the rains may seep into the dry river bed and also not get carried by the river.
>
> Conclusion is that the single project of Tehri Dam may not adversely affect the sediments because the sediments have already been created during the upstream flow or are being added from other rivers. However, a cascade of projects which prevents weathering in upstream reaches will prevent absorption of the beneficent elements in water and remove the base on which the coliphages survive. The conclusion that Tehri Dam will not affect the self-purifying capacity of Ganga waters may possibly be correct on a stand alone basis; but this cannot be extrapolated to other projects especially when a cascade is being built which will almost totally divert the upstream river waters into tunnels and prevent weathering.

Creation of coliphages

The NEERI study does not give any indication of the reasons of creation of the wide-spectrum coliphages. There is an oblique suggestion that this may be due to the miniscule amounts of beneficent radioactivity on the river water. However, this is not substantiated. If this were so, it should be possible to replicate their creation under laboratory conditions by exposing water of other rivers to same small levels of radioactivity. NEERI agreed to this suggestion for further research but expressed inability to undertake this in absence of another sponsored project (NEERI 2010).

It is possible that the vibrations of sages in the area may be leading to the creation of these coliphages. Or a unique combination of flow velocity, weathering, algae, temperature, etc. may be leading to their creation. It is wise to apply the 'precautionary principle' until we know the precise conditions under which these special coliphages are created. It is best to leave the river in its pristine conditions till then.

Algae

Riverwater has small micro-organisms that are food for bacteria. These are called 'phytoplankton'. The quality of aquatic life substantially depends upon the availability of variety of phytoplankton. NEERI has calculated the diversity indices of phytoplankton in Ganga waters. These are reproduced below:

Table 1

Average Density, Diversity and Composition of Phytoplankton at different Sampling Points of the Rivers/Tributaries in the Study Area (September, 2002 to August, 2003)

S. No.	*Sampling Location*	*Counts/ ml*	*Shannon Weiner Diversity Index (SWI)*	*Palmer's Index*
7	Tehri upstream (Bhagirathi)	0	0	0
8	Tehri upstream (Bhilangana)	46	1.55	2.0
9	Tehri downstream (Bhagirathi)	22.75	0.68	0.75

Source: Table 17, NEERI 2004.

A reading of above table shows that the Tehri upstream shows complete absence of phytoplankton and diversity Index of 0. This may be due to upstream hydropower projects which cause almost all the water of the river to flow through tunnels, deprive micro-organisms of sunlight and air that are necessary for their development.

The table also shows a major decline in the count as well as the diversity index between upstream Tehri (Bhilangana) and downstream Tehri (Bhagirathi). These data indicate a negative impact of Tehri Dam on micro-organism. NEERI has not assessed the implications of this decline. (All material in italics is from an activist's summary of the NEERI report, used with permission.)

The Phage in Ganga

It is interesting that the role of the phage as available in sediment, is the most emphatic aspect of a river's life and sustenance. Ravi Nandan Singh, in his path-breaking work on Benaras and the river Ganga (unpublished theses submitted to JNU 2010) writes of these phage as disappearing because of the irrevocability of plastic, both as reality and as a metaphor, which replaces the theological idea of the immortal soul. Singh writes that the Ganga Action Plan was set up in the domain of a particular affectual politics where Rajiv Gandhi saw his role as expiatory, after the assassination of his mother in 1984 and the criminal elimination of five thousand Sikhs (the number is disputed by activists who believe the number to be much larger) in the capital city of Delhi. To quote from Singh's doctoral work, submitted to JNU in 2010 and titled 'Representations of Death in Benaras',

> The extent of the river's pollution cannot be gauged by the abstract quantified measures of scientific results of chemical experiments or moral-religious damning of the people. The extent of the pollution can be properly estimated by locating how people's lives have been failed by liberal democracy in certain domains, water being one major component of it, but not the only one. Badiou similarly does not consider the liberal humanitarian capitalistic democracy itself as to be the evil. He argues that what is evil is that it is posed as the greatest possible Good. He also argues that Evil could only be conveyed when Good is clearly represented. Thus it would be useful to locate both these idioms in Badiou's own words. In

delineating Good he poses event, fidelity and truth to be the *three registers:*

> The event, which brings to pass something other than the situation, opinions, instituted knowledges; the event is a hazardous, (hazardeux) unpredictable supplement, which vanishes as soon as it appears; the fidelity, which is the name of the process; it amounts to as sustained investigation of the situation, under the imperative of the event itself; it is an immanent and continuing break; the truth as such, that is, the multiple, internal to the situation, that the fidelity constructs, bit by bit, it is what the fidelity gathers together and produces. (Badiou 2001: 67–68 in Singh 2010: 181)

Singh uses the work of Veer Bhadra Mishra, the mahant, who combines his religious belief with scientific principles to clean the Ganga. He writes that,

> He (the mahant) observes that the machineries installed at the ghats do not work, so the only way to 'save' Ganga would be to apply a plan which runs without electricity. In his plan of 'Integrated Wastewater Oxidation Pond System' based on 'biological control' it is a 'return to the bacteria'. (Singh 2012: 214)

Singh traces the history of the discovery of autophage to Felix D'Herelle, and others, such as Ernest Hanbury Hankin and Frederick Twort (ibid.: 220). Singh quotes D'Herelle's 1921 work,

> The difficulties of exposition of the subject will readily be comprehended if we realize that up to the present time Bacteriology has been considered as a 'problem of two bodies', bacterium and medium, whether the medium be the organism parasitized or a culture fluid. And this problem of the two bodies has been indeed complex. But it is of necessity much less complicated than the 'problem of three bodies' with which we must now be concerned, where we must recognize the interactions between the medium-culture medium or organism parasitized, – the bacterium parasitizing this medium, and the ultamicrobial bacteriophage parasitizing the bacterium. (D'Herelle 1921: 6 in Singh 2012: 221)

The interesting problem for the Sociologist is of course that the relationship of the State to it's people has changed dramatically. T.K. Oommen's work *From Mobilisation to Institutionalisation* (1985) was concerned essentially with the way in which land reforms could make a difference to how the poor benefitted, or did not benefit as much as was hoped, from *bhoodan* and redistribution. The problem of land displacement has been foremost in the minds of social scientists for the last several decades. For the generation that grew up with the idea of dams as the symbol of a secular and rational citizenship, the real problems came with the questions around the latter. Amita Baviskar writes in *Riverlines* (2003) that,

> Dams and bombs stake out the territory of Indian modernity; Nehru's temples now serve to glorify the Hindu rashtra (nation), trailing displacement and death in their wake.
>
> Sacred rivers have been profaned in more ways than one. How can one talk about Indian rivers without acknowledging their appalling pollution? Far too many of them deserve Huysmans's condemnation of the Bievre in Paris:
>
> That strange river, that dumping-ground of filth, that bilge which is the colour of slate and melted lead ... starred with muddy spittle .... The river is nothing but a moving dung-heap. (Baviskar 1993: xiii)

C.A. Rashid has in his M.Phil dissertation, titled 'Industrial Pollution and People's Struggle: A Case Study of Eloor, Kerala' (JNU 2010), argued forcefully for riverine rehabilitation. In a note he prepared for circulation, he says that,

> For the past two decades, social anthropological research on environmental issues has been part of a broad public sphere that has witnessed a sharp increase in environmental decay like, contamination of ground water, degradation of flora and fauna, genetical disordering and livelihood problems e.g decline of fishing wealth and the fertility of agricultural land, on the banks of the Periyar river due to large-scale emission or affluence of manufacturing, biochemical industries. The associated people's struggle and industrial and state discourses attract sociological investigation.

Sustainable development is the bases of the people's movements on the banks of the Periyar in Kerala, and following the pioneering work of T.K. Oommen, C.A. Rashid believes that people's movements are essentially innovative and creative. My work on the fisherpeople in Allapuzha in the 1990s showed that river and sea movements were becoming linked across India, as fisherpeople believed that they had the right to protect the earth: Tom Kocherry and the nuns and priest of the radical liberation theology movements essentially believed that they would link up with Medha Patkar in order to provide a catalyst to the Ecological movements of the 1990s to give a framework, within which grassroot leaders could represent the occupational choices of men and women in the country (Visvanathan 1994, 2000). David Harvey in the *Spaces of Capital* (2001) argues that ideology defines the way in which space is transformed in the relationship established by migration, between town and country. He writes,

> The history of cities and of thinking about cities has periodically been marked by intense interest in the transformative role of urban social movements and communal action. Such movements get variously interpreted, however, depending upon historical and geographical conditions. The Christian reformism culminating in the social control argument of Robert Park and the Chicago School of Urban Sociology (evolved during the interwar years in the United States and exported around the world in the post war years as standard fare for urban sociologists) contrast, for example with both the pluralist 'interest group' model of urban governance favoured by Robert Dahl and the more radical and revolutionary interpretations arrived at (mainly in Europe and Latin America) during the 1960s and the 1970s (culminating in Castell's magnum opus on The City and the Grassroots.)
>
> (Harvey 2001: 188)

Harvey suggests that, 'the sense of possibility and desire for change in political and intellectual circles, often expressed as utopian dreams of alternative city forms on the one hand and the need to identify political agents – such as proletariat or urban social movements – capable of realizing such dreams on the other' represent potential points of disjunction (ibid.: 189). While the bourgeoisie represent Commonwealth Games and Walmart as the symbol of their consistent desire to be westernized, the farmers' movements have essentially located the earth and their articulate position on it, in the use of symbols, as their anchoring point. When Khandwa farmers immersed themselves in their inundated fields for a fortnight till their MPs and Chief Minister responded we see just such heroism, unrelenting because farming was their life. Gandhi wrote in the 1920s and 1930s in Young India, that the poor are committed because they have nowhere else to go. Patriotism then becomes the very lifeblood of such movements. While Germany and Japan have said 'No!' to nuclear energy, the Indian Nation State pulverizes the survivors of the Tsunami in Kudankoolam, but the protest of the fisherpeople is essentially about water, pollution and right to life and work. Whether it is the 48 rivers that flow into the sea in Kerala, or the state of the Coovam as it represents the sludge of Chennai, activists have made rivers the essence of existence for both town and country. The rivers are the veins of the cosmic egg, the seas the inner waters, as Diana Eck reminds us.

Was citizenship a basic human right? The difference between the rhetoric of the 1950s and the loss of dialogue in the 21st century is because there has been a radical shift away from the redistribution model to the idea of the liberal economy, where the bourgeousie get to make the rules, regardless of political party. The obstacle to a shining India, or to the development paradigm are the farmers, the rural stakeholders in agriculture. The State's interest in agriculture then, unfortunately for such people, as farmers with small land holdings, becomes represented as Food Security, Scientific Temper, Industrialization of Agriculture, Bt technology. The ideology of capitalism then locates itself in the questions of ruling the masses, the so called 80 per cent of our population, which now is drawn into the cities as cheap labour during floods, famines and drought. The riverine economies which are ancient and self-sustaining are now problematized as essentially out of sync with the real ambition of Indians, which is colonization of extra terrestrial space, and missile warfare, as the art of hoarding, self defense and power mongering.

In a talk given at Centre for Historical Studies, JNU on 14 September 2012, at the Sarvapalli Gopal Memorial Lecture, Christopher Bayly spoke of the friends of Nehru who influenced him, and these were G.B. Pant, A.R. Gadgil, Mahalanobis, and Radhakrishnan. Pant brought the sense of village India, influenced as he was by Malaviya and Gokhale; A.R. Gadgil believed that co-operatives were a mid-way towards industrialization; and differed in this from Gandhi, who believed that rural development was an end in itself; Mahalanobis was concerned with the ethnographic role of the State, and Radhakrishnan thought that Vedanta could bring people appreciably closer (Bayly 2012). There is another map, though, I wish to argue, and that is the way in which we understand how the Congress Socialist party in the 1930s, brought about a great dialectic in the way we think about peasantry. This was essentially to use associations and the printing press during colonialism to actually work a new map of rights and duties for the farmers, which would include wages, prices and consumption. These *kisan sabhas* as Acharya Narendra Dev saw it, were an integral part of the vision of how the peasantry would define it's own place in the birth of the nation. In a paper written for presentation at the Benaras Hindu University at the Exclusion and Inclusion Cell in 2009, I argued that today, the farmers need to define their orientation to land, water resources and food in terms of the debates which make them representative stake holders, in how India is perceived by them (see Visvanathan 2009). The theoretical premises which were discarded in the tension that arose between the CSP and the Congress during the freedom movement have to be revisited. An 'intelligentsia of the people', which is essentially what activists are, have to present the very terms of the argument in terms of the practicality of their world views. Freire encourages Scientists to learn from the people.

The right to life, and the right to speech is one of the key areas that the activists who fight for Gangajee and the free flow of her waters define as the primary aspect of their struggle. However, given the vested interests of the MPs, MLA, traders and their goons, the activists who wish to oppose the building of dams for Hydroelectricity have a very hard task. When Bharat Jhunjhunwala was attacked in his home, the activist Vimalbhai sent out a petition, on 26 June 2012. His first language is Hindi, in which his blogs are written, but for the benefit of English speakers who do not read Hindi, he wrote as follows,

> Dear friends
>
> as you know about the attack on Bharatji by goons of dam company. as many of us are active and doing something in different way. now i think there is need of a coordinated effort or divide the work. I have some thoughts in my mind which i am sharing with you.
>
> Petition to NHRC on the roll of state government (need to make a draft, i am trying to find out possibilities form lawyer)
>
> mass letter writing to CM and to PM my letter is with you, English translation can be done.
>
> Delegation to power Ministry – demanding black list the company and contractor
>
> Delegation to MOEF asking them to follow their own rules and committee recommendations. (on a larger issue related with dams on gangaji we can work on that)
>
> letter or a Delegation to PM as he is the chairman of NRGBA with all the member of NRGBA
>
> statements form different district of Uttarakhand (i am doing that and some other groups are also active) Best vimalbhai

The blogspot matuganga.blogspot communicates the urgency of the matter. In 1942, when Gandhiji came out of jail, he communicated that the cotton farmer could survive only if he/she learnt to multi-task (ibid.). They would have to be spinners, weavers, dyers, and also learn to sell their cloth. The activists of the river protection communities are essentially learning that if their concern with wholistic living is to be the signature of their life and work they will have to be visible, not just numerous. The interesting aspect of the bourgeoisie is that they cannot see the people, except as functionally in servitude to them. Popular movements dispel the idea of the invisibility of the masses, as the peasants of

Khandwa and the fisherpeople of Tamil Nadu have shown with regard to nuclear energy which potentially and vehemently changes the horizon of their daily lives. The Gandhian prerogative of 'doing without' becomes the leitmotif of these movements .... It is a choice they make, and as citizens they have a right to those choices. When America returned and state decorated Dr Jhunjhunwala, a former faculty member of the IIM, who chooses to live in a village in Uttarakhand, writes to intellectuals, petitioning for support, he says,

> Many dams on Ganga River have been held up because the Supreme Court has asked for a study of cumulative impacts of dams on river ecology. Now Ministry of Environment and Forests has given a study to IIT Roorkee. Our study indicates that this study will be a whitewash. We have written a note on he topic which is attached for your kind perusal. We intend to circulate it widely among all faculty members of IIT Roorkee, and more. We have sent a similar note to Ministry of Environment and Forests already. We would be very happy if you would endorse this petition and also help us obtain endorsements by academicians past and present – and persons who can help us.

J.P. Debral, one of the intellectuals who was asked to mediate between World Bank officials and activists' opposition to WB loan wrote on 7 April 2012.

> Come what may. We will have to accept reality. RR issues will remain the most important issue for the affected people. This is also sure that once they get the money many of them will not oppose the dam. But then they have nothing to loose if they oppose the dam after getting the compensation. Let us keep this opportunity open. Let them say what damage has happened or is likely to happen after taking the compensation. We cannot be choosers at this stage. We will have to continue to fight at every front. Those who are opposing the dam at the ground should be encouraged to do so. The dam authorities or the government must face resistance from every quarter. We cannot be selective here. If Bharat Bhai wants to interact at the policy level we must encourage and support him. He is doing it at the Rajya Sabha, Planning Commission,

> Courts, WB and Government levels. Every level has to be dealt with. I think Vimal Bhai, Madhu Kishwar, Bharat Bhai and Thariyalji have already made their positions clear. Let us respect their commitments. I do not want to pitch the wisdom of one against that of the other.
>
> Together we can think of bringing change. A few inches gained by each of them will make a feet of progress. What is important that in the end the policy changes. Regards J.P. Dabral

Activists have their perspectives which arise from their orientations and training. Biographically, they may have points of departure. The energy that one person has is a result of many hundreds of people in the movement, providing him/her with a stabilizing position. Weber's theory of charisma as a form of social action is useful for us to understand, since activism often depends on the power of the collectivity to recognize this individual as a catalyst for social change. The networks that form may run in time span of decades, as in the case of Tehri, including in its fold, new members according to context. On 10 December 2011, an activist wrote that,

> We had filed a Writ Petition in Uttarakhand High Court, regarding the Dhari Devi Temple, which is to be uplifted for Srinagar project. The High Court asked us to approach Archaeological Survey of India. If ASI fails to protect the monument then we may approach the HC again. The temple is not currently protected under the Ancient Monuments Act. Please let me know if you know someone in ASI who can help.

Elsewhere, in my work *The Children of Nature* (2010) I have shown how secular scholars and devout believers have engaged with the question of the greening of the Annamalais and specifically the Holy Mountain, called Agnisthal or Arunachala, in Tiruvannamalai, Tamil Nadu. The Madras High Court has accepted petitions on behalf of Arunachala, thought to be the embodiment of Shiva and Parvati in unison. So also, the concern that believers have shown in the protection of Ganga is allied with the concern of ecologists, scientists and activists of various political hues. When Bharat Jhunjhunwala was attacked, the noted activist Vimalbhai sent a letter to share the pain of the event, on 25 June 2012

Dear friends

You might know on 22nd June 2012, a mob of about 40 people including employees and contractors of JVK, a company building a large hydropower dam in Uttarakhand, India, barged into the house of Environmentalist Dr Bharat Jhunjhunwala and threatened him to withdraw his legal representations against the dam. This is a breach of personal safety, freedom of speech and democracy. The Government of Uttarakhand must ensure that perpetrators of this attack are brought to courts and tried. The administration so far has taken no initiative to arrest them. Law and order in the state remain at the mercy of Political leaders and powerful police officers. Daughter of Dr Bharat Jhunjhunwala, started a online petition to gather support for his right to lead a knowledge-based agitation in favor of his beliefs.

We all friends of Bharatji support this petition. The support from all the concerned citizen is not only solicited to support and declare solidarity to Dr Jhunjhunwala but also the cause to protect the fundamental right of 'Right to Speech'.

The attack against the Bharatji is not only against that particular individual but in fact this is an attack to suppress the voice of the people in favour of environment and peoples rights by the dam builders. The attack shows the attitude of total disregard of environment issues and peoples rights and the dam builders want to construct the dam with any hook and crook.

(http: //www.avaaz.org/en/petition/Action_against_attack_on_Environmentalist_Bharat_Jhunjhunwala/?fRgZjdb&pv=0)

We request you to spare some time to read this petition to Chief Minister of Uttarakhand state in India and sign to support the cause.

Vimalbhai and Rajendra Negi – Matu Jansangthan Visit our blog<matuganga.blogspot.com> some films on youtube, just type – bandh katha For Correspondence only: D–334/10,

> Ganesh Nagar, Pandav Nagar Delhi–110092 We associate with National Alliance of Peoples' Movements (http: //napm-india.org/)

The whole process of building opinion to save sacred rivers takes time, energy, money, and involves legal help and publicity. Yet, those who care about the legacy of a 5,000 year civilization, often feel they have the time and the commitment of the people who dwell in these riverine communities. In that sense, they are optimistic, because their notion of time is not apocalyptic, it is essentially ordered by their faith either in the divine or in the rational secular order of the Constitution as it is enshrined in the common knowledge of ordinary people. Activists seek to rewrite the contexts of modern geography by the play of interstices in how cartography becomes an emotional space for these actors. To the reified space of maps as authoritatively represented as an idiom of the nation state, they use local grammars and everyday practice to rewrite the plans of centralized government. This affectivity is seen to be essentially problematic, and is voiced or represented by partisans of Nation State and local communities in different ways. 'Do you think Development will not happen' asks one side acerbically 'just because the jholawallas do not want it?' On the other hand intellectuals who are concerned with the rights of peasants and tribals to speak in postmodern democracy will write on the behalf of local communites. Maps are therefore not just artistic productions (see Baviskar 1993) explaining where places are, their contiguity to forests, lakes, mountains and railway lines, but as Dodge et al. argue (2009) in their book *Rethinking Maps*

> Maps do not then emerge in the same way for all individuals. Rather they emerge in contexts and through a mix of creative, reflexive, playful, tactile and habitual practices, affected by the knowledge, experience and skill of the individual to perform mappings and apply them in the world. This applies as much for mapmaking as for map reading. As such, the map does not represent the world or make the world' it is a co-constitutive production between inscription, individual and world; a production that is constantly in motion, always seeking to appear ontologically secure. Conceiving of maps in

> this way reveals that they are never fully formed but emerge in process and mutable (they are re-made as opposed to mis-made, mis-used or mis-read).
>
> (Dodge et al. 2009: 21)

Jane Beckett, while describing the transformation of the rural landscape in the 19th century in Netherlands, through industrialization, shows that its museumization was an ongoing process. She writes that the transformation involved both the diversification of agriculture under capitalism as well as the use of fertilizers and pesticides replacing animal manure. Potatoes replaced the small scale garden, where vegetable production and dairying had previously been standard livelihood practices. In Kerala today, where small dams have been accepted by the people, the State Government has made it very clear that the people must have recourse to agriculture even though the lands lie fallow due to migration for work in Gulf Countries, Europe or America. Shaju Philip writes, 'Last week saw politicians up on arms over a suggestion by Planning board Deputy Chairman Montek Singh Ahluwalia that Kerala not worry about food security but instead focus on cash crops. His suggestion must have been prompted by the large tracks of paddy fields lying uncultivated in the state for years because of lack of labour hands – both outward migration from middle class agri –families and shift from food crops to cash crops hit the fields.' (Philip 2012: 20) The Kerala politicians however know that the State's interest in organic farming as expressed in the success of Ezhimayur in Pallakad has to be reduplicated in other parts of Kerala. (Visvanathan 2009) The political position represented by all parties, including the ruling Congress party that the State is not ready to hand over to monopolists is a legitimate claim to make. Beckett writes that 'Michel Foucault has noted that 'a whole history remains to be written of spaces – which would at the same time be the history of power … from the great strategies of geo-politics to the little tactics of habitat.' (Beckett 2001: 64)

The moral claims that people make to the past may involve geological time, and mythic time, as well as the way in which industrialization can make a famine struck, drought prone, water logged in the monsoon desert like Barmer in Rajasthan, suddenly turn into an oil field, with luxury hotels and modern roads, with farmers selling off their lands rapidly, or conversely mythographers continuing to search for the River Saraswati. The polemics of industrialization may suddenly replace the mythological impetus, and this is something that Sociologists urgently need to work on, since their task is essentially that of documentation and analyses.

Note

1. This was mentioned by scientists of NEERI during personal discussion with Dr Jhunjhunwala, at NEERI on 18 February 2010. This is not mentioned explicitly in the two NEERI reports.

References

Baviskar, Amita, 1995, *In the Belly of the River*, OUP, Delhi.

Baviskar, Amita (ed.) 1993 [2003], *Riverlines*, Penguin Books, Delhi.

Babu, J. Manoj, Shamal Mandal, Bandana Mahto, and Sudha Goel, 2011, *Emerging Contaminants in Ganga River Basin with Special Emphasis on Pesticides* (internet report).

Beckett, Jane, 2001, 'In the Bleaching Field: Gender, Landscape and Modernity in the Netherlands 1880–1920', in Steven Adams and Anna Gruetzner Robins (eds), *Gendering Landscape Art*, Rutgers University Press, New Jersey.

Eck, Diana, 2003, 'Ganga: The Goddess Ganges in Hindu Sacred Geography', in Amita Baviskar (ed.), *Waterlines*, Penguin Books, Delhi.

Dodge, Martin, Rob Kitchin and Chris Perkins, 2009, *Rethinking Maps*, Routledge and Kegan Paul, Abingdon and New York.

Ghatwai, Milind, 2012, 'The Means to Block or Release a Dam', *The Indian Express*, 19 September.

Harvey, David, 2001, *Spaces of Capital: Towards a Critical Geography*, Edinburgh University Press, Edinburgh.

Irschick, Eugene F., 1994, *Dialogue and History: Constructing South India, 1795–1895*, OUP, Delhi.

Jevtic, Miroljub, 2007, 'Political Science and Religion', *Politics and Religion Journal*, Vol. 1, No. 1.

——, 2008, 'Religion and Relations between Genders', *Politics and Religion Journal*, Vol. 2, No. 1.

Mackenzie, A.T., 1899, *History of the Periyar Project*, Government Press, Madras.

Mines, Diane P. and Nicolas Yazgi, 2010, *Village Matters*, OUP, New Delhi.

Oommen, T.K., 1985, *From Mobilisation to Institutionalisation*, Popular Prakashan, Bombay.

Pandian, Anand, 1993, 'An Ode to an Engineer', in Amita Baviskar (ed.), *Waterlines*, Penguin Books, Delhi.

Philip, Shaju, 2012, 'Why FDI Retail No-Go in State That Earns Well, Spends Better', *The Indian Express*, 19 September.

Rashid, C.A., 2010, 'Industrial Pollution and People's Struggle: A Case Study of Eloor, Kerala' (unpublished MPhil dissertation, Jawaharlal Nehru University, New Delhi).

Raju, Suvrat and M.V. Ramana, 2012, 'Where the Mind is Full of Fear', *The Hindu*, 19 September.

Singh, Ravi Nandan, 2010, 'Representations of Death in Benaras' (unpublished PhD thesis submitted to Jawaharlal Nehru University, New Delhi).

Visvanathan, Susan, 1994, 'The Fishing Struggle in India', *Seminar*, November.

——, 2000, 'Workers of the Sea', *Seminar (Annual)*, January.

——, 2009, 'Foresters and New Orientations to Survival', *Indian Journal of Human Development*, Vol. 3, No. 1, January–June.

——, 2010, *The Children of Nature: The Life and Legacy of Ramana Maharshi*, Roli Lotus Press, New Delhi.

——, 2010a, 'Forestation and New Educational Practices in Living Together, Symposium on Intercultural Dialogues: Problem Posed by Ramin Jahanbegloo', published in (610) June 2010. Indian express web page 30 August 2009 New Refineries likely in Barmer.

Index